the
Build It
Brilliant
Blueprint

Take Your Business Online in 4 Simple Steps.
A Book for Helping Professionals.

by Zoe Thompson

Contents

Chapter 1

Welcome

"You need to just get started. If you never get started, you'll never be successful."

- Justin Kan

Welcome to the wonderful world of online creations; the opportunities to share your expertise with the world are exciting, endless and easier than you might think. If you're here I know the time is right for you to explore the online options and I'm here to help you every step of the way. It's time to share your expertise and create a sustainable business, there's never been a better time to do it. Let's get started.

Introduction

Most people in the helping professions are wonderful, trained professionals who have the skills to help change people's lives, but they struggle when it comes to marketing and 'the business side of things,' leaving them working long hours for minimal return.

The world is struggling with pandemic levels of stress, anxiety, trauma, obesity and ill health and yet 3 in 5 helping profession style businesses fail to make it past the first 3 years. A fact that seriously frustrates me. Imagine what a difference we could make to the world if everyone learnt how to build a brilliant business! It was this fact that was the driving force behind creating Build It Brilliant.

In this book I'll share with you my Blueprint, a 4-step structure to help you harness the power of online technology to achieve your income and business goals. I'm going to highlight where the methodology behind my Blueprint fits within our modern world, how you can use it to build a sustainable business and how it can help you avoid many of the frustrations and mistakes of setting up and growing your business.

Understanding how this Blueprint can help both your business and yourself will help you to implement the Blueprint successfully. My aim is that by the time you've finished reading this book you'll be excited by the opportunities and able to implement them into your business effectively. With this book I aim to save you time, money and frustration by providing you with practical exercises so you can build the Blueprint for your own business. You can also keep this Blueprint in mind and keep referring back to it when making business decisions in the future. I want your business to thrive for many years to come and for you to feel confident both in yourself and your business decisions so you can use online technologies to get out there and help people who need you.

It's time to define a strategy and structure which enables you and your business to thrive and together we can have a huge and positive impact on the health and wellbeing of the world.

Are you a helping professional?

There are so many different words which describe people who work in these kinds of professions. Ultimately what defines us is that, through our services, we help people to feel and be better in some way. You may call yourself a therapist, a health professional, a consultant, a wellbeing expert, a professional coach, a personal development specialist, a fitness expert and/or define yourself by the many different job roles within these fields. For this reason, I use 'people in the helping professions' throughout the book to refer to anyone in these professions.

Are online solutions right for your business?

If you have picked up this book and you are looking into online solutions you've probably come to the same conclusions I did. Most of us start off by offering our services 1-2-1, a business structure which leads to a few challenges. I've defined what I feel are the 3 main ones below. And, if you're finding any of these resonate with you, then online solutions and my Blueprint can definitely help you.

Challenge 1 – Attracting clients

You feel like you're spending most of your time trying to attract clients and no matter what you do it just doesn't seem to work. You've come to the point where there just aren't enough hours in the week to do everything and to see the number of clients you need in order to make the amount of money you wish to make. I find this is true for so many people so if you feel this way you are certainly not alone! I'm here to tell you it's not you, it's your business structure which is the problem. This book will give you so many 'aha' moments which will allow you to break free and finally build a brilliant business that allows you the life that you want.

The second part of the attracting clients challenge is when you hear 'I wish I'd done this earlier' from many of your clients. Perhaps, like me, you find this so frustrating and you want to encourage more people to speak up and ask for help. You know that there are people who would benefit from your services, but there seems to be a block in terms of them actually booking with you. You have a driving passion to help people and yet it feels like it is a really big leap for your potential clients to book a session. There are millions of people suffering in the world so how can you encourage more of them to reach out and make a change? If you're feeling like you have some wonderful knowledge to share and want more people to feel comfortable in asking, this book will help.

Challenge 2 – Repeating yourself

Do you find that you keep saying the same things to clients over and over again, from the first enquiry, to the consultation and right through your sessions? You've said these things so many times that they now roll off your tongue without you even thinking about it. If this resonates with where you're at in your business, there are opportunities to automate parts of your process using online technology and don't worry, there is a way to do this and still maintain a high level of service and authenticity!! This way you can stop sounding like a broken record and focus on the really important bits.

Challenge 3 – Making a difference

You have dreams about making a difference within the world but at the moment there's a limit to how many people you can help. You want to help more people, but your current business structure doesn't allow you to do so. Having a business structure based on 1-2-1 services allows you to help a very limited number of people. Perhaps you have a waiting list for 1-2-1 services and really don't want to let people down, or you have an idea/plan for a membership or course so you can share your expertise with a wider audience, but you're not sure where to start. This book will help you to build a business structure which allows you to expand your reach but not by becoming a "busy fool" and/or losing your integrity.

If you are experiencing any of these challenges in your business, it's time to look into how online solutions can simplify your life and help you generate an income that gives you a thriving business without you having to work every hour God sends.

So what exactly is the Blueprint going to help you do? It will help you to harness the opportunities of online marketing and online learning to:

a) find a simpler, more effective way to market your business
b) make a positive difference for a larger number of people

c) design a business which allows you more freedom and time
d) create a structure which enables you to achieve your income goals

Many people in the world of the helping professions realise that using online solutions have lots of potential but they struggle when it comes to what they should do, how to do it and how to price their creations. Whether you are just starting out or ready to grow your existing practice this book will help cut through the overwhelm.

By the end of the book you will have a 4 step Blueprint for your business. So if you:

- feel overwhelmed by the many online options and want to know what's right for your business
- want to know how to avoid the mistakes
- would love the put yourself out in the world more but feel scared and find yourself procrastinating
- already have online solutions which aren't making you money and want to understand why

You are certainly not alone, and you are in the right place. In this book I'll share my personal experiences, along with my learning from building my own successful therapy business and from helping others in the helping professions to implement a successful online strategy. My aim is to cut through the overwhelm, inspire your creativity and help you to build a brilliant business.

There is no shame here, I've made the mistakes, tried (and failed at) lots of things, lost money and overcome my own inner confidence gremlins and I'll talk about them all in this book.

In-person vs online sessions

Before we move on and I tell you a little more about my background, lets tackle one of the biggest concerns people have when taking their helping profession business online. I find this particularly relevant to those who identify as therapists, but I've also heard it discussed amongst others. It's a debate which has been ongoing for years, are online sessions as effective as seeing clients in person?

When you are sitting in a room opposite another person there's an energy and a connection, and many professionals worry that they won't be able to deliver the same level of service via online means. One particular element of concern is the level of observation, an integral part of any assessment and diagnosis. The therapeutic alliance, or therapeutic relationship as it's also called is such an important part of any successful outcome so people are concerned about creating and sustaining that interpersonal connection online. Add to this concern about connection issues, technology failure and the ability to fully connect in an online space and many people are led to believe that online solutions won't be as effective.

Having done many face-to-face and online sessions in my career I completely understand these concerns, but I do think online sessions have a lot to offer. Here's three reasons why:

Number one, technology has improved a lot in the last year or so and with a little forward planning you can protect your relationship with your client and deal with any technology issues, issues which are getting less and less frequent.

Number two, online sessions can open up opportunities to those who wouldn't be able to visit you in person e.g. creating reasonable adjustments for those who experience barriers in accessing your in-person service, such as those who live in rural areas or have medical restrictions which prevent them from travelling.

Number three, thinking only about online sessions is an example of black and white thinking. The possibilities of online technology are vast and, thinking this way inhibits your creativity and opportunity. Online technology has so many possibilities, delivering your sessions online is only one of them. What about:

- using online technology to encourage people before they get to your chair?
- using it for providing additional learning or support outside of the room or between sessions?
- supporting people who just can't afford the cost of one-to-one face-to-face sessions?

When we open our minds to the many opportunities technology provides, we can create a customer experience which helps many more people enjoy better lives. I have personally heard time and time again people in the helping professions say they don't want to take their businesses online but what they really mean is they don't want to deliver their sessions online. This is black and white thinking in a world full of colourful opportunities and it inhibits your creativity before you've even got started.

Having said this, what does the science say about online sessions? Are they effective? Online therapy is an emerging field, there's definitely more research to be done but early outcomes are positive, showing that online therapy is a viable alternative. Here are three studies which have already been published:

In this <u>2014 study published in the Journal for Affective Disorders</u>* they conducted a randomised study of 62 people and found that online sessions for depression were as effective as face-to face.

In this <u>2014 study published in Behaviour Research and Therapy</u>* they studied the effectiveness for online Cognitive Behavioural Therapy for people with anxiety and found that online sessions were cost effective and had positive impacts at a one year follow up.

In this <u>2018 study for Cognitive Behavioural Therapy published in the Journal of Psychological Disorders</u>* they found online sessions is 'effective, acceptable and practical health care.'

Our world is changing, the global covid pandemic of 2020 meant that people in the helping professions had to stop their face-to-face sessions. Instead, many decided to experiment with the online alternatives. The overwhelming feedback I heard was that people were pleasantly surprised by the results. The vast majority enjoyed it and felt their clients' outcomes weren't negatively affected. With a little extra planning, such as ensuring the client created the right atmosphere at home and knew what to do if their connection was interrupted, the sessions were just as good. The pandemic has also significantly increased the number of people who are now comfortable with using online technology, a move which will enable more people to access the help they need and reduce the amount of

*http://bit.ly/bibref1 *http://bit.ly/bibref2 *http://bit.ly/bibref3

hand holding you'll need to do.

Having said that, online sessions aren't for everyone and that is absolutely fine too. All I ask is that you reserve your judgement and have a mind open to the possibilities, this way you can build a business which is right for you and your clients.

Why do 3 out of 5 businesses fail?

A little while ago I attended a conference and one of the speakers shared that 3 out of 5 therapy businesses fail within the first 3 years. This figure, although astounding, didn't surprise me. At the time I was trying to keep my head above water, I was being a very busy fool trying to build my business.

At first the figures for a 1-2-1 business structure appear to add up, £60 an hour is a much higher hourly rate than I was on in my corporate job so I should be able to earn more money, right? This is exactly the thought process I had when I first started but unfortunately something was drastically wrong because the figures just didn't add up.

Burnout is cited as one of the main reasons why so many businesses of this kind don't survive. From personal experience I know what this feels like. It feels like you're on a hamster wheel and you can't get off. No matter how hard you work you just can't make the maths add up.

I put this level of failure rate and burnout down to the following two factors:

1) A helping professions business needs constant new clients to keep it going and gaining new clients is the most expensive and time-consuming way of

attaining business.

2) Support for therapy/consultant style businesses isn't too forthcoming and normal solutions just don't fit.

Let's go into each of these factors in more detail.

Factor 1

In our professions we heal people, we make people feel better. If you are successful in your job your clients will go off and lead healthy and happy lives, so you will need a constant flow of new clients.

As a one-woman business I found that my marketing strategy and £60 an hour business structure didn't allow me to earn what I needed. I've included a working example below to explain what I mean.

Working Example:

Let's say you wanted to earn £20,000 a year personally after expenses. So, your business would need to make more to cover your expenses which would then leave you with £20,000 for your income.

NOTE: I know many people who work with clients weekly and I also know many who work with clients over longer so for this example I've used 2 weeks as an average but feel free to adjust the figures to suit your current business model.

So, let's say you have a turnover of about £35,000, which would work out at business expenses of £1250 per month (that's everything, rent, system subscriptions, tax etc) to leave you with your £20,000 per annum income.

Many 1-2-1 services in my experience charge £45-£60 per hour, let's be generous and work with £60 per hour for this example.

So, £35,000 divided by £60 = 583.33 hours a year. Divide by 52 weeks = 11.2 hours of client work each week (let's say 12 for ease).

Presuming you see clients twice a month, 12 x 2 = 24 clients per month in order to make the £35,000.

Let's say that on average each client has approx 3-6 sessions so they will be a client for 3 months.

You would need 24 <u>new</u> clients signed up each quarter to get 12 hours of client work per week so you can personally earn £20,000 a year.

The Problem: Not everyone you meet is going to buy from you, conversion rates are way smaller than you think!!! Attending your local networking group 3 times a week isn't going be enough to convert 24 new clients, let alone feed your continuing need for an additional 24 every quarter.

NOTE: Conversion is what we call the process of taking someone from first contact through to actually signing up to something with you.

I'm not saying that this business structure doesn't work, I have a few colleagues who have made it work. I'm just saying that this business structure is really hard work and, in my opinion, definitely a leading factor in why 3 out of 5 of these businesses fail.

NOTE: This also means that if you wanted to earn more than £20,000 a year, you'd have to either see more clients or increase your hourly rate. I also haven't given you any weeks off in my calculations!!

This is the main business structure I see when working with people in the helping professions and there are a number of problems with this:

- Your income is capped, there are only so many hours in the day so only so much you can earn.
- Therapy work is demanding physically and mentally: seeing lots of clients each week is hard work.
- It requires you to do the legwork of finding clients and often there aren't enough hours in the week.

Also, depending on your profession it can be easier or harder to convert clients e.g. private physio clinics will probably convert easier than hypnotherapists. This is because most people understand the concept of a physio, they can receive referrals from the NHS or be funded through health plans and insurance. Hypnotherapy isn't understood by the general public and isn't accepted in the vast majority of countries as a mainstream service. Depending on your profession it may be easier or harder to convert 24 clients each quarter.

I hope from this you can see why building a helping

profession business purely on 1-2-1 services with you doing the marketing is a very hard and costly business model to sustain.

Factor 2

Now, let's look at factor 2 in more detail. Support for therapy/consultant style businesses isn't too forthcoming and normal solutions just don't fit.

Local authorities and councils offer support to new starter businesses, so long as you're not a therapist/helping professional one-person microbusiness. Our style of business falls through many cracks and in my experience (which is based in the UK) often it doesn't fit the criteria for grants, funding, business support etc. If you do manage to qualify for support with websites, marketing etc, which I have done over the years, the solutions tend to be designed for bigger businesses with bigger budgets and just don't fit. They are over your budget, not aligned with the helping professions or too big for your needs.

This is one of the big reasons why I set up Build It Brilliant. I was sick of investing in things which were meant to be my ticket to success only to find out they didn't work for my business.

When I launched my therapy business Refreshed Minds in 2011 with £750, due to my financial constraints and my business structure, I had to do it all myself from building my website, creating leaflets, setting up newsletters, creating and editing videos, building online courses, creating e-books and more. This all eats into your time each week which then makes the finances problem I outlined in point 1 above even worse.

I found that there simply weren't enough hours in the

week to see enough 1-2-1 clients, learn everything I had to learn, market my business effectively and do all the admin tasks to keep my business going.

And the biggest struggle of all, countless times I felt alone and as if nobody could help me.

I wish that I'd had this Blueprint when I started out, it would have saved me so much stress and helped me to build my brilliant business much quicker.

Working through this book will help you to ask yourself the right questions so that you can create a solid business structure on which you can build specific online pieces. Online solutions which will actually enable you to reach your goals without the burnout!

Chapter 2

Why would you listen to me?

"If we do not remember those who have gone before us, we are destined to repeat the same mistakes. We walk blind through time."

- Kate Mosse

Your business should be a blend of your particular skills and passions (you'll learn more about this later in the book). It took me a long time to figure out what mine were, but I've finally got there.

My unique and eclectic blend of skills and experience make Build It Brilliant what it is, they are my passions and the things I care about in the world. These are:

1) I am an entrepreneur who set up with £750 and built a therapy business of my own.
2) I am a self-confessed tech geek with 10 years of experience creating training and e-learning for multinational companies.
3) I've worked in the service industry since I was 16 - helping people is in my blood.

I love blending my passion for the helping professions and my passion for technology to help you to build a brilliant business.

These three things I feel are paramount to what makes me, me. Next I'll tell you a little bit of my journey to discovering each one.

Finding my love of technology

I'm one of those strange people who gets excited when a new app is launched, who spends hours playing with software to see what it can do. I've always been this way; I get it from my father who has always had a passion for the latest gadgets. On a call recently a therapist joked about the cupboards in my studio saying he imagined that when you opened the doors loads of tech would fall out. They weren't wrong, that and a lot of books!!

It was the 5 years I worked in Learning & Development designing and delivering training with a particular interest in e-learning that cemented this love. In those days it would cost about £300 to commission a video, so myself and a colleague could frequently be found bringing in our video cameras, Mac computers and microphones from home so we could put together training. We pushed PowerPoint to its limit, and I found my love for creating exciting and interesting online learning.

In my business I've integrated my e-learning knowledge with my therapies. Ever since I started my business in 2011, I have created videos, online worksheets, courses, audios and programmes for my clients. I thought this was what everyone did but slowly others started asking me to show them how to do it. It's funny, isn't it, that we don't really notice what we do differently, until someone else points it out!! To me creating online stuff is so normal, I didn't have a clue that people would not know how to do it and might want me to help them.

Along with my 1-2-1 clients and corporate work I was helping other therapists and consultants to take their businesses online and they found success doing it. I created ad-hoc courses and delivered them to those in my circle who wanted the help. They loved my enthusiasm, my straight talk, my creativity and my ability to make what they thought was a complex subject feel easy and exciting.

For 3 years I sat on the idea of combining my love of therapy and my love of technology. Like so many others I thought nobody would be interested, that life was good so why rock the boat, and that solutions were already out there so the world didn't really need my voice. I ignored the niggles and carried on. For 3 years!!!! Yep, I made excuses and told myself it wasn't worth the effort for so long that I believed it.

But in February 2020 I decided to formalise the idea into something real, I launched Build It Brilliant in March 2020. About 2 weeks later the Covid pandemic hit and what I thought would be a soft and slow growth hit the ground running as everyone wanted to know more about the online world. I'd found my calling and I loved it right from the start.

Finding a love of mindset and therapy

Twice I've left the job which I thought I wanted to chase a dream of something better.

The first time I rebuilt my life was in 2006. I left my job managing a 150-seater restaurant with 27 members of staff, my 9-year relationship and my home within 3 short months and I moved back into my mum and dad's house at the age of 25. I remember driving back up the M6, it was my birthday and I had everything I owned packed into my Ford Focus, I felt I was a complete and utter failure.

I didn't know what was next, I just knew somehow it would work out OK. From this I learnt that sometimes big leaps take lots of courage and faith. What I didn't have at this point was a mindset toolkit to help me transition through these difficult changes in my life. Little did I know that 18 months later my lack of knowledge was going to bite me in the bum.

I stayed with my mum and dad for about 6 months and then I landed a dream job and moved to Leeds.

About 18 months into my new job as a Learning and Development Consultant I crashed. I was suffering from debilitating stress, but I didn't know it was that at the time. I was diagnosed with IBS and just about held it together enough to continue working. I was exhausted, shaking, fearing everything and feeling nauseous every single day. I was a mess. Through a friend I found a hypnotherapist and was amazed by the difference hypnotherapy made. I understood so much more about myself, my brain and how the changes over the previous 2 years had impacted me. I became fascinated by how and why people do what they do.

Over the years that followed I've qualified in NLP (Neuro Linguistic Programming), Hypnotherapy, Coaching and SIRPA (Stress Induced Recovery Practitioners Association). I have a passion for the changes that the helping professions can make to people's lives. The world needs people to shine so others can overcome, survive and move through their lives to a better understanding of themselves and how they operate within their world. It deeply bothers me that the world is experiencing pandemics of stress, anxiety, illness and suffering, yet 3 out of 5 businesses who have the ability to help are failing!!

So, what was the second time I rebuild my life I hear you ask, well that was in 2011. I was sat in a meeting room with my manager at my corporate Learning and Development dream job listing all the reasons why I "should" be happy. I had the job I thought I wanted, with a team of amazing creative people, the salary, the pension etc etc so why was I desperately unhappy? I'd been there about 5 years and now every day I would sit at my desk getting more and more frustrated with the politics and day to day expectations of corporate life. People kept telling me to wait for redundancy, but I was too restless.

After that fateful meeting I went home and finally decided to take the plunge, handed in my notice and set up Refreshed Minds with about £750 in the bank. This was the second time my life would be rebuilt from the ground up, but this time I felt I had the mindset tools to manage it well. I still remember people calling me mad, brave and wishing me luck - with that look in their eye that says, "what the hell is she doing? She'll be back".

I can happily report that I have not suffered any major mental or physical downsides this second time around, but I did face a very different challenge. I didn't know a lot about building a business back then and at that point I didn't realise how much I didn't know. Fast forward, a lot of tears, a lot of struggles (a lot of which I'll share with you in this book) and I've turned Refreshed Minds into a successful business.

So many therapists I've met and supported over the years have felt the same as I did. They have a yearning to make a difference in the world but feel scared to take the plunge. My experiences have taught me that it's OK to feel scared to step out into the world and show it what you're made of. If you feel nervous about starting your new business, scared of appearing on camera or hesitant about writing your true thoughts in a blog. I completely understand what it's like to take a leap of faith and do something because you feel it's the right thing to do.

Even though I have cried and threatened to pack it all in and get a 'proper' job hundreds of times, I still don't regret leaving something I didn't feel was right in search for my dreams. The journey has allowed me to realise who I am, what I bring to the world and I'm really proud of myself for everything I have managed to achieve. I don't think I could have the same level of self-awareness and mental strength if I had decided to stay in the corporate world and I certainly wouldn't be half as good as I am at supporting you and doing what I do today without all of that experience.

My ethos of service

I can't leave this chapter without sharing with you the third passion which shapes who I am in this world. It's one of the reasons I finally decided that the world needed Build It Brilliant. It's my experience and ethos about service.

I started my career in the catering industry. Over the years I did everything from bar work to managing a 150-seater restaurant. I have always loved connecting with people through service. This is probably why the current online world annoys me so much, I don't feel it really fits anyone with service at the heart of what they do. With landing pages which are overly salesy and marketing which feels like it's more about how much you can sell than the people you're selling it to. It doesn't fit with my ethos. When you genuinely care about people the way I do so many of the marketing tricks feel like you're saying, 'this is me, buy my stuff' and it's the equivalent of welcoming someone into your restaurant and slamming a plate of food in front of them. That is not service!!!

True service is an art, a dance of communication and the focus is on taking a genuine interest in the person in front of you. I want to encourage this within the online world, showing you how serving your clients and sharing your expertise authentically online can work together to create the income you want.

I now bring my whole experience to your business. My love of technology and my love of serving people to bring together something exciting which you'll enjoy creating and your clients will love consuming. I understand what it's like to step into the unknown with only blind faith and a dream. I genuinely love holding your hand and supporting you to build your courage every step of the way.

Step aside boring online programmes, step aside overwhelm and confusion, together we are going to build something brilliant!!!

Why now is the right time to step into the online world

The world of online marketing and online learning has seen some momentous changes over the last 20 years. For many years during childhood we didn't have mobile phones or the internet but these days you can shoot, edit and distribute a video from anywhere with a mobile phone.

Online technology is now more accessible than ever, with apps, software and virtual reality, there are so many options to help you to connect with your audience and share your expertise with them, a fact which means that many who start on this journey feel overwhelmed.

This book is written to help you cut through the noise and decide on a solution which is perfect for you and your business. I'm a great fan of minimalism and it isn't just about buying a small house!! It's about choosing simple solutions which work brilliantly rather than cluttering your life with too many things. Creating a successful business which uses online solutions effectively is just the same. Let's not have you spending hours researching the best tech and creating things which waste both your time and your money. Instead let's spend a little time working through the exercises in this book so you can have laser-like focus and maximise your opportunities online.

Online technology has become so much more intuitive than it once was: you used to have to install software and then read a 300-page manual to know how to use it (trust me I've read quite a number of them!!). Now, you click and play, software is built for the common man not someone with an IT degree and you can find help easily online. Solutions have also come down in price, for just a few hundred pounds you can have a professional looking studio to record your videos. You no longer need to invest £1000+ in a professional camera, your smartphone is perfectly good enough.

So, the world of online solutions is now in the hands of the everyday person within a realistic budget that you can afford. Along with access to the technology, the internet has given us the possibility to connect with people around the world with a click. There's never been such a great opportunity to share your knowledge with those who need to hear it.

Here are some facts and figures. By 2022, the global e-learning industry is projected to surpass $243 billion (Statista) and digital learning is the quickest growing market in the education industry, with a whopping 900% growth since 2000. KPMG have predicted a continued rise for the next 5 years. The covid-19 pandemic has forced businesses to rethink online working and it's a trend which is set to continue. The online world is now more accepted and understood than ever before, it's a great time to take advantage of what's available and discover how you could benefit from being a part of it.

And what about your ideas and dreams?

So many helping professionals have some wonderful ideas, but that is what they stay...just that, an idea, locked away in their heads and never being shared with the world. You know you could reach more people, that you have amazing ideas, and that the technology is out there to help you do it. But you stay stuck. Stuck because you don't know how to start, stuck because you don't know how to turn that idea into reality, stuck because you lack the confidence to get out there and do it.

The world is suffering from pandemics of stress, chronic pain, anxiety and fear - people need you!! You may think there's so many voices out there already and that there's no room for yours, but there are 7.5 billion people on this planet, that's enough for everyone to have their slice. Perhaps your idea could be just the thing someone is looking for...

You can sit, feeling stuck, thinking everyone in the world is better than you, or you can decide that your dreams are just as worthy as anyone else's and go for it. The choice is yours.

How can this book help you?

Here are some of the most popular questions people ask me about online solutions:

1) should I focus on creating videos?
2) should I be blogging?
3) should I be creating an online course or a membership package?
4) what should I charge people for my webinar?
5) how do I market my practice?
6) I've heard about podcasts and want to start one, any tips?

If any of these resonate with you I would, with great respect say you're asking the wrong type of questions. Answers to these questions and more will become obvious when you have the right foundation and structure. But, in my experience this isn't where people begin their journey with online technology and they rarely spend enough time thinking about the foundations and structure of their business.

I want to help you avoid spending hours creating content that nobody buys or wasting money on technology you don't really need. I want to help you work smarter not harder so you can create the life you want.

So, if you feel overwhelmed by technology, or you are not sure what you should be creating, you'd like help to create something amazing or feel you're procrastinating and fear failure, then the Blueprint I take you through in this book will be the clarity you need for your business.

This book will help you get those ideas out of your head and into an actual structure, using this structure you can then focus and build specific online pieces knowing exactly why, who it's for and how to price, market and talk about them. I call this structure my Blueprint and I'm going to take you through it step by step in this book.

The Blueprint is a 4-step structure and it will help you avoid all of the mistakes I've talked about so far. The Blueprint will help you save time and money, so you won't be a busy fool and spend hours and hours creating something which people don't buy. It also gives you an opportunity to explore your creativity so that you are excited by what you are going to create. I want you to build a business that is sustainable, profitable and allows you to achieve your dreams. The Blueprint will help you do all of that.

And, you are no longer alone. I'm here to help you through the minefield that is online technology and guide you step by step so that you can step up, take advantage of the online opportunities and share your wonderful ideas with the world.

Introducing The Blueprint

Here is the Blueprint in its entirety, it consists of the following four parts,

1. Foundations,
2. Environment/Market,
3. The Structure
4. Roof

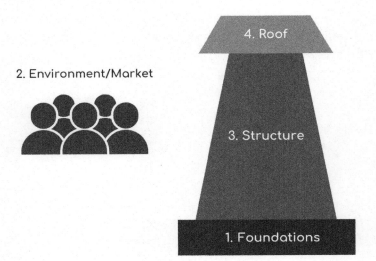

Over the next few chapters, I'll take you through each of the steps - providing you with exercises for each. These exercises will help you to build each part of the Blueprint for your business. The Blueprint is a business jigsaw puzzle so you can play with each of the elements individually until they all fit together into something which makes sense. For example, you may decide on your foundations but then choose something in your structure which doesn't quite match and need to return to review your foundations again. I recommend doing each of the sections in turn but keep an eye on your business as whole as you do so. You may need to keep coming back to certain ideas and playing with them until you find something which fits together nicely.

Also, please keep in mind that you are a human and not a robot, some of the exercises may take you a while to work through because they trigger your thoughts or need some mental time to process, that's absolutely fine. If you need to, take time to absorb the information and use this book as an ongoing working reference. My aim when writing this book was for it to become one of your go-to books, a book which has been well thumbed through, devoured and one that provides a continual source of ideas. It truly doesn't matter if you take time to work through it or you read it straight through from cover to cover and then implement your own ideas.

Everybody who reads this book will be at different points in their business journey so I've tried to include options and ideas which will suit no matter where you are. I've also included a number of downloads along the way so you can use those if you wish or just find yourself your own notebook and pen.

If you find the ideas in this book stimulate your excitement for the online world and feel you would benefit from some more help as you work through your Blueprint, join my Bib membership programme. You can find all the details here: http://bit.ly/Blueprint-Resources

The membership is a great way to chat with others as well as receiving support from me.

Okay, let's get into the Blueprint.

Chapter Summary

The Blueprint is a combination of my passions of technology, mindset and service. It provides you with a structure you can use to implement online solutions effectively into your business. Remember that no expert becomes that way overnight, they were all once at the beginning of their journey too. It's only through learning, practice and dedication that you become good at something. This book can help you uncover your passions, answer all of your burning questions about online technology and support you in creating a business which is uniquely you. The Blueprint is made up of 4 sections, the foundations, the environment/market, your structure and the roof. I'll be going through each of those individually in the chapters to come.

Chapter 3

Foundations

"The problem with competition is that it takes away the requirement to set your own path, to invent your own method, to find a new way."

- Seth Gobin

No successful business was built on wobbly foundations. Get these basics right and everything else will fall into place. Luckily the foundations are just two exercises, so it won't take you long to find clarity and apply these within your business.

When I started Refreshed Minds back in 2011 I was excited to get out there and find people who would want my services. I looked around to see what the 'going rate' was and found that most people in my area charged £60 per hour. I thought, 'I'm happy with that' it was a lot more per hour than my corporate job!! Since it was a therapy style service, I didn't want to charge my clients for more than they needed, so they would pay me for each session as and when they came. So that was that and I went out into the world to see who would buy my services.

I have seen many therapists and consultants who do exactly this, time and time again as a therapist and also as a clinical supervisor - when I ask "how much do you charge?" the answer is "X number of pounds per hour and people pay as they go". So, what's wrong with that I hear you say.

This type of business structure creates a few problems. The first one I realised at the beginning of 2016. It took me a while to admit it, but my business wasn't doing very well. I was exhausted and financially scraping by. My husband and I decided to take a mortgage break for a few months to ease the pressure. As I've mentioned earlier this 1-2-1 business model is the costliest and most time-consuming way of doing business. You reach out to new people, give them a number of sessions till they are better and then move onto finding more clients. I didn't realise just quite how much time is required to seek and acquire new clients.

What I came to realise was there weren't enough hours in the week. I was constantly out networking, doing social media videos and spending money on marketing. When I sat down and worked through the finances, like the example I gave you earlier, that £60 per hour didn't look so great. I couldn't make the time to find new clients and the time to serve them and then make any type of decent money.

The other problem with this business structure is that people pay for each session when they come. You are relying on their commitment and their understanding of what's best for them. Both of these things that humans are notoriously not great at...! You'll get a few people who are committed and take your advice, but most will say 'oh I feel better now, I don't need you', even though you know that one more session would mean long lasting change. You look at your week and it's full, only to find that people cancel, cancel, cancel for a myriad of reasons and you are left eating baked beans on toast for the third night running wondering where you've gone wrong.

We need to build a business which enables you to work smarter not harder and we need to start with you, so that you feel motivated and can build something which is in line with your needs.

So, how does this fit with taking your business online? Well, firstly you need time to create those wonderful videos, programmes etc and secondly you need to create a structure which allows you to earn the money you actually want to make.

Your options online are endless, you really can design your structure in a million different ways. So, without the Blueprint structure in place many people struggle to decide what they should create. They end up with lots of ideas and doing none of them. I spoke about these questions earlier e.g. should I create an online course or a membership package and how much should I charge? If these types of questions resonate with you and your business, you haven't got your foundations in place so this is where you should start.

Answers to these types of questions become obvious after you've worked through this foundation chapter. Once you have your foundations in place you can test each of your ideas against your answers to these exercises - to ensure you're choosing the options which are right for you.

Your business has to start with you, what are your dreams, what kind of money would you like to make etc. Only then can you build a business which allows you to achieve them. So many therapists and consultants don't do this, they just look at what the competition is doing and just do that. I did the same because I was scared of getting it wrong and when I started out, I didn't know better. I want you to know better.

Go through each of the exercises below and give yourself permission to decide on what you would like to create in the world. It's OK if it going to take you many steps to get there, at least you'll know each choice is in line with what you want, as well as what you don't. Having this understanding in place will allow you to reach your goals much quicker.

It's easy to look at the competition and think that they know best, then get locked into a business which you don't really want. It's also easy to put your head in the sand and not do these exercises in the hope that it will all work out in the end. I encourage you to take some time to go back to your foundations and ask yourself, what is it that you want and then start from there.

Time and money

Part 1 - Time

This first exercise helps you to avoid the trap I fell into of being a busy fool and instead maximise your output, i.e. your money, for the amount of time each task will take you.

What we're aiming for here is deciding on a total time figure indicating the total amount of hours you can dedicate to your business each week. This time includes doing your books, doing your admin, networking, getting back to client enquiries etc etc. In our world the price our clients pay needs to cover ALL of our business hours. Not just the ones when you're actually physically helping them.

We are going to look at our time in two ways, firstly we'll look at your current reality and then we'll look at an ideal future you'd like to aim towards. If you know these two figures already great, just note those down so you can refer to them as you build your structure. If you haven't got them yet or think you know but haven't actually decided or written an number of hours down, work through the following exercise and make sure you have two definite figures you can work with before moving on.

Why do we need to do this before decided on what online product/programme to create?

Most people just think about their online ideas and get straight on to making them a reality. I urge against this approach and here's why.

CASE STUDY:

A counsellor contacted me and asked if I could help her with some online ideas for her business, she was thinking about setting up a Facebook Group. I asked her why a Facebook Group, she said she'd been reading up about marketing and read that it was a good way to build an audience.

My first question was how much time do you have to spend on your business each week? What are your current commitments? She had about 25 hours per week and she has two young children. A Facebook Group is a very labour-intensive thing to build, you need to be in that group posting content and helping people to engage with your group daily. There are now hundreds of Facebook Groups so building an audience from scratch is tough. This counsellor worked with people on all sorts of issues including bereavement.

With this approach she'd be asking people to talk about really tough things in their lives in an open forum with others. I'm not saying that won't work I'm saying it's a hard and labour-intensive way to build an audience. For someone with two small children and a counselling business to run, it's not the solution I would recommend.

Understanding how much time you have to dedicate to your businesses allows you to choose an online structure which fits with the time you have available, thus avoiding busy fool syndrome. For this counsellor I suggested a video series instead. She could set time aside to record the videos and create the structure and then sell it over and over. Much less time per week and a much easier way of getting people engaged in her topics.

The other reason why this foundation chapter, and deciding on your time commitments, is so important is that most people run their businesses with a never-ending to-do list. They try to do too many things and end up feeling like they can't complete anything. Leaving each day with a to-do list still full of a million things you haven't done yet just saps your motivation, creativity and energy. Imagine what it would feel like to know that everything you needed to do fitted into your week. Wouldn't that feel nice? By knowing your time commitments, you can decide on tasks which fit, allowing you to do everything each week without feeling like you 'should' be doing more. Working smarter not harder is our aim.

"Zoe has a wealth of knowledge, skills and experience. I always come away with new ideas or a new perspective to approach my goals."

- Marisa Walker-Finch, Counsellor

Step 1 – Where are you now?

Firstly, we're going to look at your life as it currently is so that we can see how many hours you have to work on your business now. Think about your week and consider these questions.

1) What are your current commitments other than your business, how much time do they realistically take?
2) Do you have certain hours where you can focus on your business e.g. evenings, during the day etc?Is there anything currently which you could stop doing to give yourself more hours?What are the things you would like to do but don't currently have time for?

After taking into consideration all of these things and looking at your current commitments, give yourself a realistic number of hours per week that you can you spend on your business along with any constraints you have identified.

Don't worry if that's a small number, we can build your business, so it fits. It's more important to be realistic rather than to over promise and put unnecessary pressure on yourself.

Now what a lot of people do here is to then divide that time by their hourly rate and think, 'oh that makes a great sum, I'm happy with that'. BUT, what about all those tasks you need to do which aren't client facing hours? When are you going to create these wonderful online e-books, courses etc? When are you going to plan to do your social media? What if you could make that money in 4 hours per week instead of slaving away seeing 20 clients? We need to think smarter here so for now just stick with the total hours figure and we'll build a fantastic business which fits those hours as we go through this book.

Step 2 – What is your ideal?

Now let's look to the future and the kind of life you would like to build. Whilst this isn't the time you have available now, it can certainly help you to choose online things which won't hinder your ability to achieve your future dream.

CASE STUDY:

I ride a motorbike and I've always wanted to go off for a month at a time, travelling. After all, you can only get so far from the UK in 2 weeks. But originally, I built a business based on 1-2-1 clients. This business structure actually hindered me achieving my dreams. My diary was full of 1-2-1 clients who needed me, clients who need to see me often for a long period of time. Whilst at the beginning I was enthusiastic to get out there and make a difference in the world, over time I lost my motivation and felt a low mood creeping in. It drove me crazy because I got a lot of satisfaction from my client work but deep down, I resented it. I kept dreaming about something which I felt I could never achieve.

This is the problem with building a business before you think about what life you want to create. You could end up creating a business which actually hinders your dreams. Having your longer-term goals in mind can help you to make more informed choices.

Now I choose to create online courses which people can buy and work through, and I choose to collaborate with other experts within my membership, that way I can fulfil my dream. Currently I can't make my dream trip come true because my hours are spent building my business, but I know that whilst I'm doing that my decisions will still support me to get there. If a new opportunity comes my way, I can make a decision based on whether it will take me closer to my goal or further away. Having this in mind helps me to achieve those goals quicker.

So, what are your dreams? What kind of things and life would you like to work towards? In the future how much time would you like to dedicate to your business?

Here are some questions which you might like to consider:

- How much time would you like to spend on holiday, does 2 weeks suit you or would you, like me, prefer a different work/life balance?
- What about your family commitments, aging parents, growing children? Will the amount of time you have to dedicate to your business change and if so how?
- Would you like to stay hands-on or would you like to have other people do the work for you?

It took me ages to finally say that what I wanted was important. I spent years serving everyone else, doing what was expected of me or, more to the point, doing what I thought was expected within my industry. The idea of actually creating a business which suited me was an alien concept for a very long time and it may be for you too. Perhaps this is the first time you've realised that it's okay to want what you want? Perhaps this is the first time someone has said you can build something your way? I encourage you to spend some time thinking about what you want, free from other people's well-intended opinions. If you could create something which you love, what would it be? Spend some time thinking about what would make you happy and what kind of 'work' you would like to do.

As I've mentioned already when I started out, I just looked at what everyone else did and did that. I would ask endless people for their opinions before making a decision and I didn't trust my own instincts when it came to business decisions. The things I liked doing were often an afterthought e.g. if I got everything else done, I could spend an hour with a friend helping them create their online course. Now I laugh about how pleasing I was, how my entire life and business was built around these perceptions and how I never gave myself the credit or the opportunities to build the life I actually wanted. Please don't do it this way!!!!

I'm here to let you know that that your dreams matter, that your ideas and voice matters. It's OK to make decisions about your own life and then build a business which serves you and creates the life you want.

Oh, and this doesn't have to mean a mansion, a boat and a million pounds. Personally, I'm not a materialistic person, I dream of grand things but in reality, I'm most happy sitting with a tent, around a campfire and good friends. It took me years to decide that my version of reality was good enough and I don't have to want what other people say I should want. Phew!!! Now I'm free to create the life I want, and it feels so good to focus on that.

So, ditch the expectations and the money driven commercialism which don't serve you and decide what is the life you really want?

Now how many hours per week/type of working week would you like to aim for within your business?

You can grab a notebook and scribble down as you explore your ideas, or I've created a little Time Worksheet you can download. http://bit.ly/Blueprint-Resources

Deciding on your two figures for this exercise may take some time to formulate, don't worry if you keep coming back and refining it over and over. Whilst I could quite easily write down a figure in hours for both of these it probably took me a year to finally give myself permission to say yes to the things I really wanted. I would write something and then realise it was someone else's version of success. Eventually, I wrote things which were honest for me and I didn't give a dam what other people thought so don't give up and know that you can come back to these figures and keep refining them as often as you like.

Part 2 – Money

Many people I work with are afraid of money. They don't know how much they've got or how much they need, they seem to cross their fingers and hope that the sums work out at the end of the month. I've never been this way. This way of interacting with money is alien to me.

I remember when I was little sitting down at the table with my mum helping with the family finances. She had a simple spreadsheet; one column had a list of all the money going out and the other a list of money coming in. The table would then be littered with papers. We'd sit together going through the papers and update the spreadsheet. At the end she'd ask if there was anything we were missing, and we'd chat about what we should do with any money we had saved or left over. She always talked to me about savings and what we were saving for - there was money set aside for Christmas and money set aside for any holidays. It was an activity I looked forward to and I still have a spreadsheet for my household finances now.

What this taught me was good financial management and not to be scared by money. In fact, I enjoy knowing what's coming in and going out, I don't fear my accounts each month and I know exactly how much my business costs me. I thought that this was just normal, until I realised that most households don't have a spreadsheet or anything like it. I have no idea how they cope!!!

So, I encourage you to get clear on your household and business finances, sit and look through those receipts, get them in date order and create some way of seeing what's coming in and going out each month.

I know this can be scary, but you need to know what you're dealing with before you can start creating the business you want. Working hard and not knowing what you've got financially from doing all that work is disempowering and feels like more of a struggle than it needs to be.

Step 1 – Household Finances

I advise you to start with your household finances, this way you know how much you need your business to bring you each month.

So, your first task is to go through your bank account and create a way to see your household finances simply so you can keep track of them. This may be by creating a simple spreadsheet, I've created a template for you to download if you would like one, or via an online solution such as Starling or Monzo. The aim is for you to clearly see the amounts currently coming in and going out.

This may take you a little while so put down the book, go and do it and then come back. You will thank me for it I promise.

OK - Now that you've got a clear picture of where you are currently, we are going to look at 3 figures. Open your household finances spreadsheet and work out the following 3 figures:

1) Your get by (Need) figure,

    How much money per month do you absolutely need to earn from your business in order to get by? This doesn't mean to be able to buy a new car or have a lavish holiday. I mean, to have a roof over your head and some food on the table. A basic, I-need-this-amount-to-survive figure. Don't worry about how much your business costs you to run at this stage, business costs are variables, we can add those on to give you your turnover figure. For now, just write down how much money you NEED to take out from your business each month to survive.

2) Your happy (Want) figure,

    How much money per month would you like to earn in order for you to feel happy and comfortable? To have a little luxury and know that everything is covered with a little to spare. This may even be what you're earning now - often we don't realise that we're doing OK and give ourselves permission to notice it and feel proud of ourselves.

3) Your OMG (Wish) figure,

    How much money would make you feel amazing?

If you could earn this per month you would be financially secure and have enough to spoil yourself. You would feel like you have achieved something brilliant, and it would make you smile every time you looked at your bank account.

Write down these three figures next to your hours per week figure from part 1.

You now know that within x number of hours per week you Need, Want and Wish to earn x amounts of money to fulfil the criteria.

A note about mindset

You've heard the saying, 'where your attention goes your energy flows' right? Well this is also true for your money. For years I had my focus set on achieving my 'get by' figure so guess what, that's all I ever achieved. Each month if I earned that amount, I would feel good and think I'd done well. Then I'd set about the next month to do the same. My thoughts were that that was the figure I HAD to earn, so I made it my mission to make that happen.

The minute I realised this is what I was doing and then set my target to my Happy figure I started making small adjustments, mostly unconscious ones, and guess what my income started increasing. Not right away but slowly it moved.

It matters what you mentally focus on, so be careful with where/what your inner voice aims for.

So why do I ask you to know your get by/need figure if you aren't going to focus on it? Some people aren't even earning what they need so it depends on where you are within your business. Setting a realistic target which you feel comfortable with may start off with your need figure.

Also, whilst you are mentally aiming for your 'happy' or 'OMG' figures you will need to make decisions to build and grow your business. Every decision comes with an element of risk and by knowing your 'get by' figure you know the base level of income you need to survive, so you are more likely to protect it and less likely to go below it.

It is absolutely OK to build a business which matches your needs and dreams. Read that sentence again and again if you need to. It took me a while to allow this to sink in and finally give myself permission to decide on my own money/time figures.

It's also worth mentioning that there is an audience out there for every price point so don't hold yourself back because you have fear around selling at higher prices. Online technology has endless opportunities, and the Blueprint will help you to bring it all together. At this point you just need to know your time and money foundations figures.

By defining these time and money foundations you also avoid ending up being a busy fool and building a business you don't actually want. Create a business which allows you to make the money you want to make in the hours you have available. As you work through this book set your mindset on a figure which you feel is achievable but will make you happy, then we'll work on creating the structure that matches it.

If you want some great reading material to understand money mindset, overcome your blocks and have some extra support I've listed some of my favourite reading on the topic of time and money in the extra resources section: http://bit.ly/Blueprint-Resources

CASE STUDY

In 2015 I started working with the UK and Europe's leader in psychophysiological disorders (PPD), Georgie Oldfield from SIRPA Ltd. At the time Georgie was running physical training courses for health professionals around the UK and as well as seeing clients in her own clinic and online, she was traveling to London every month to run a clinic there. Both Georgie and her husband had ageing parents and she wanted to be able to have the choice of being able to spend time with her family when they needed her.

Together we created interactive and engaging online

courses for her Practitioner Training. We also created a membership to provide recurring income and moved all her consultancy sessions online. This has given Georgie the freedom to work from her family's homes across the UK or even in her motorhome if she chooses. It's also given her more stability which has enabled her to take time off when it is needed. Georgie's business continues to thrive with the addition of an online Mindbody Wellbeing Series and an online group Coaching Programme this year which was launched to support people during the pandemic.

"Zoe began working with me just at the right time as I was beginning to realise that I wanted to have more flexibility and freedom with my work and therefore I needed to look at my work and consider how I could streamline it and move every-thing online. Zoe was instrumental in helping me make the re-quired decisions, as well as supporting me practically, as we made the major step of moving everything online. Over the past 5 years Zoe has become an integral part of the organisation and is involved in every major decision and change made."

- Georgie Oldfield MCSP

Finding your Passion

The next part of building strong foundations is to think about what drives you and fuels your motivation. A brilliant business will require your continuous effort for years to come, there will be great days and tough days. There will be hurdles to overcome and your patience will be tested over and over again. It's your passion and motivation which will keep you going when things get tough.

Sure, you can start a business based on something you think is a sound business decision, but your happiness, motivation and sense of being will be higher if you tap into something which also feels congruent and worthwhile for some bigger purpose than just yourself.

Now passion and motivation alone don't ensure the success of a business but when you feel something is worthwhile and purposeful energy radiates from you and people are drawn to want to get involved.

You need both passion and sound business decision to come together and that's what this first exercise can help you to do.

Ikigai

One of the big pieces of wisdom I'd like to share is the Japanese concept of Ikigai, roughly translated this means 'reason for being.' It has long been thought that this is the concept behind a long and happy life and since work is a big part of our lives, it makes sense to build a business which also fits into this framework.

Ikigai is a great concept which you can use to define your business, as it ensures you're choosing something which you're passionate about AND makes sound business sense.

Below is the diagram of Ikigai:

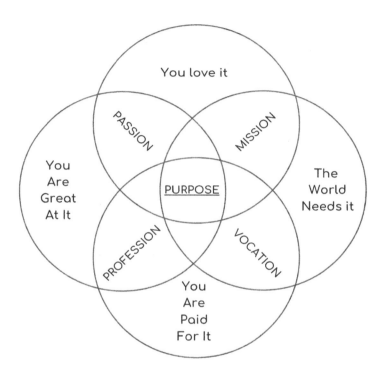

You don't have to start at any particular point of this diagram and no one of the four elements are any less or more important than the others.

Think about the business that you want to build and ask yourself:

1) Do you love it, do you have a passion for it?
I find a simple way to determine this is to have a con-

versation with someone about it. If your face lights up when you talk about it, if you could talk about it for hours and still not feel tired, if you feel invigorated after the conversation…. you have found a passion.

2) Would people think you are great at it?
Be careful here, we are notorious for selling ourselves short. This isn't about comparing yourself to the great people of your industry (we can always improve our knowledge). This is about comparing yourself to the people who will be in your audience, who you want to serve. Would they think you're great? Do your friends come to you for help with it? Do people seek your advice about it etc. If the answer to these questions is yes, you are great at it, even if you think you're not!!!

3) Will people pay for it?
Setting up something you're passionate about that nobody will pay you for is a hobby. A business requires money, so you'll need someone to pay you for what you do. Thinking about what you have/want to offer…. is this what people are willing to pay you for?

4) Does the world need it?
This is a question about saleability. If the world doesn't need what you are offering it's either morally wrong, against your values or not worth bothering to create because nobody needs it. Are there people out there who know that they need precisely what you are offering?

THE purpose vs A purpose?

So many people I talk to struggle with this idea of finding their purpose, they feel they need THE purpose and procrastinate waiting for some lightbulb moment of clarity to come crashing into their realisation. It's an idea I also struggled with for a long time. What nobody told me is you can change it. What a revelation!!!!

You don't need to find THE purpose, you just need to find A purpose, something which you feel is purposeful. This model stops you making dumb decisions such as creating an ice cream business in the north pole, extreme example I know, but you get the idea.

Loving what you do isn't enough but equally creating a sound business which you don't love isn't enough either. Use this model to choose something which does both, a sound business decision and a decision which you feel excited and passionate about.

Your purpose will change as you grow older, learn more about yourself and develop your understanding of your industry and that's absolutely fine. Don't let your quest for finding THE purpose cause you to procrastinate so much that you never get started. Just choose something which feels right for right now and build a business structure around that. You can add to it, take things away or change it if you feel your purpose changes but at least you know you'll enjoy it along the way.

Chapter Summary

Having strong foundations enables you to make informed decisions about the business you want to build. It allows you to create a business which matches the number of hours you have to spend with the money you want to earn - preventing you from being a busy fool. It can feel scary to finally decide that what you want is important and face the reality of the financials, but it's also liberating and enables you to create a business you actually feel excited about. If your business doesn't match your needs and dreams for the future what's the point, you might as well go and work for someone else. After working through these exercises, I hope you're feeling those strong foundations beginning to form. We'll keep referring back to these as we go through the book to ensure you build the business structure which matches the choices you've made here.

Chapter 4

The Environment: Choosing your customer

"You can't transform something you don't understand. If you don't know and understand what the current state of the customer experience is, how can you possibly design the desired future state?"

- Annette Franz

n step 2 of the Blueprint we look at the environment/ market. Who are you actually going to serve? This is another area which I feel most people don't think about before deciding on the online solutions they're going to create. Instead, people spend weeks creating online programmes and then going out to the market only to be greeted by a tumbleweed of silence. This usually means their marvellous creation sits gathering dust and sometimes the author declares that online solutions don't work.

Don't worry I've done this too in my time, you are not alone!! But now, using the Blueprint and the exercises in the following chapter I am going to help you to avoid these mistakes or at least rectify them, if you already have wonderful creations which didn't sell. I completely understand why the mention of 'market research' and 'understanding your customer' sends shivers of dread through your body, it did for me for many years, but I'm going to make it a lot more relevant and useful.

Sitting in a beautiful, vaulted-ceiling upstairs conference room I stared at an 'ideal client' worksheet trying to fill in the boxes but struggling. I can't tell you how many times I've done this activity and each time I've found it hard. Who is my ideal client? What's their age? Are they male/female? What's their annual income etc. Most of the time I've just stared blankly at the boxes, thinking about my clients and the fact that the clients I like working with are from a mixture of genders, places, backgrounds etc so who do I choose? This has been the same experience every time I've entered information into those boxes, and I can honestly say I don't think it's made any difference to my business.

I get the premise of the activity; you can't serve everyone and by trying to, you actually serve no one. Better to 'niche', choose an audience and focus something on them, that way you're connecting with them, speaking their language and attracting them to your business. Yes, this makes absolute sense to me but the questions on the sheet never helped me to do that.

In my opinion, I think the classic structure of the 'ideal client' worksheet makes it lose its credibility. The questions just don't portray the power of the idea or allow you to harness its potential into something which is usable.

In this next section I'm going to harness the power of this activity, because I do understand that by serving everyone, you're serving no one, but instead of the usual 'pick an ideal client worksheet' I want to make it more applicable and implementable to your business.

Here are a few of the difficulties/mental struggles I found when doing the traditional ideal client worksheet:

At the beginning I don't think I was ready to choose an 'ideal client', I wanted to see what clients I enjoyed working with, so I resisted the exercise completely and never actually decided to focus on anyone. If you are new to your profession, I completely understand the logic behind this thought process. If this is where you are it's OK, but you are currently researching your business, you are not yet ready to build a brilliant one.

There's a difference between making a business decision to-niche, or not-to-niche, and choosing to serve whoever comes in your door because you don't know yet what you want to do. I know it's frustrating when you first start because you want to be successful but please have patience, research is an important part of your journey to success. It takes time to gain experience by serving clients so you can decide what you like and don't like and you'll hone your business and your skills by doing so. Don't give yourself a hard time because your business isn't growing fast enough or delivering the money you had in mind, these things will come in time.

If you are further along your business journey, feel like you're clearer on who you'd like to work with and think it's time to look into the business decision about niching I talk more about that later in this chapter.

I wish when I started out someone had explained that difference to me. I spent ages fussing and anxious over the niching/not niching decision when really, I didn't have enough experience to choose. I should have allowed myself time to enjoy researching, working with different people and finding what I liked and didn't. Instead, it felt like everyone expected me to have known who I wanted to work with from the start, which I didn't, so I felt like I was doing something wrong.

It's OK to do your research, work with a bunch of different people and decide what you like and don't like. Just know that this is where you're at and what you're doing. During this stage avoid spending money on a website which you can't update, opt instead for something which you can make changes to at no extra cost. Also avoid spending lots of money on marketing one thing, instead choose to spend a little on lots of things and test, test, test, until you find something you really like. Then build a brilliant business based on what you've found you like and what works.

If you have been running your business for a while and still feel resistance to this exercise perhaps you, just like me, have this foolish notion: I felt that if I completed the 'ideal client' worksheet and actually chose, I would then get stuck serving dark haired, middle-aged, solicitors. I get bored rather quickly and I quite liked the variety of people walking through my doors and I wanted to keep it that way. So, I sat pondering over the exercise and never actually chose anyone. The challenge with this is that I ended up trying to serve way too many people and nothing I created particularly resonated with anyone.

There is a far better way of harnessing the good in this exercise: instead of age, income etc I'd like you to ponder over the following ideas and create an environment/market you'd like to serve. Instead of concrete facts about your 'ideal client.' I urge you to get a really good understanding of the people who you want to serve.

Creating a journey

The important factor is to take your customer on a journey and to serve them. If I want help with something, I want you to take me from the start to the end, on a logical journey through to a solution. Don't create a bunch of blogs or videos on different topics each week with no clear next steps for your customer to take. This is confusing, it leads to a lack of trust and people don't buy from you.

Too many businesses do this, they just put together 'stuff' about their ideas and different helpful things, then put them out there asking, 'do you want this, maybe this, or what about this?' There is no strategy behind what they are creating. This makes you a busy fool, creating lots of things and not really marketing or getting anywhere with any of it. You feel like you are a failure because nobody wants to buy what you are offering. I've been there, don't worry but it's not you that's the problem, it's your strategy!!!

As you are thinking through the questions below think about taking the client on a journey and serving them every step of the way.

Remember to keep in mind your foundations, remember you want to be able to serve your customers well, in line with your passions and the time you have available to serve them. You want your blueprint to come together, so if your choice of customer don't match your foundations, keep playing with the pieces until you have something which fits together.

Who is your environment/market?

So, you need to make some decisions about your business. Who are you going to serve? Who are you going to take on that journey through your business? Who are you going to help?

Here are some questions to help you identify your customer. I'll then go into each one in more detail.

1) To niche or not to niche? Do you have a passion for people with addictions and want to propose a range of offers for that person? Or do you want your business to do one thing but support different

people e.g. you support people with building confidence but you help people from different sectors?

2) What keeps your people awake at night? What is it that they are worried and frustrated about and want the answers to?

3) Where do they live? Do you want a business which is just focused in your local area? Or the country where you live? Or do you want your company to be worldwide?

4) What is common in that marketplace right now? What are people buying and are there any gaps which those clients are looking for?

We'll now take these questions one at a time and help you to work through them for your business.

1 – To niche, or not to niche?

I find people worry about making the wrong choice here so please know you can create a successful business with either of the options I mention. You can also add to it as time goes on, so this is less about making THE right choice, more about making A choice that feels right. Take some time to think about the options but please do make a decision. This way you can focus your efforts and give your business a structure you can work on.

Often people start off with too many options, they are trying to please too many people and get lost in all the things which all those people need. They get swamped by the options and find themselves busy doing lots of things but not making any progress. This is a 'many to many' business structure but we want to avoid that because there is only so much of you and you only have so much time.

You could niche your whole business e.g. only work with teachers or you could niche your products e.g. choose different markets and offer them one product. The choice is yours and I'll go into each option in more detail below. The most important thing is to serve the client well.

To avoid the overwhelm choose a 'one-to-many' or a 'one-to-one' structure.

Option 1 – Same business (one) to different markets (many).

Examples would be

-   a counselling service who works with grief (one) and offers that to children, families and corporations (many).
-   a bid-funding consultant (one) who works with charities, corporate companies and social enterprises (many).

In this example you have a one-to-many business. One service offered to different markets. You also want to be careful with how many markets you offer your services to - you're going to need to create a cohesive customer journey for each one. Think about your foundations, how much time do you have, how much money do you want to make? Don't choose too many and then try and serve them all, as this results in the busy fool issue we looked at earlier. You want to spend your time wisely and we are aiming to work smarter not harder.

If you created a cohesive solution for each market, how many markets could you realistically serve well in the time you have available?

Option 2 – An option of services (many) to a single market (one)

Examples would be

- Working with anxiety, grief, depression, self-esteem and confidence (many). Offering services to children (one)
- Working with social media, websites and SEO (many). Offering these services to Coaches (one)

This is another example of a one-to-many business structure but instead of offering one service to multiple markets, here you're offering different services to the same market. Remember you want to create a cohesive journey for each of your services so don't offer too many and then try to keep up. Start with a few and build up as you go.

Option 3 – A particular business (one) to a particular market (one)

Examples would be
- Helping teachers (one) with stress (one)
- Supporting men (one) to improve their relationships (one)

These are examples of a one-to-one business structure. You may think that this is too small a market for a successful business, but it really depends on how much time you have and how much money you would like to make.

You can absolutely make either of these styles of business work. There's plenty of stressed-out teachers and plenty of men struggling with relationships. You may need to play with your locality to make this work e.g. a local solution may not give you enough scope but an online option for a UK market might.

How does this compare to your current business model? Are you offering multiple services to multiple markets and not getting anywhere? Do you feel like a busy fool trying to spin far too many plates? Have you chosen a niche which isn't in line with your foundations and doesn't allow you to make the money you want? Perhaps you've been thinking about niching, but you're scared you'll not be successful.

We seem to have this notion that the more we offer, the more likely we are to be 'successful' and in my experience this doesn't work in reality. The challenge is often quite the opposite, trying to do too many things so there is no focus and/or no clear journey for any specific customer.

To create a brilliant business, choose a business structure which is achievable and makes sense to your audience with a clear journey from start to finish for your clients. Many-to-many business structures can become overwhelming and unfocused, they can also cost a lot of money to market as the money is split between different markets and different services. If you don't want to niche your entire business, niche your solutions so that each one is speaking to a particular market or customer.

Remember, you don't have to decide on a niche and stick to it forever, you can start with one product or customer, create something amazing for them and then add another one.

Niching is about choosing something which is big enough for you to earn the money you want and offering cohesive solutions so that you are taking that customer all the way through the journey.

If you are qualified in a range of things the niching decision may seem a little harder. For example, I am qualified as a hypnotherapist, a coach, a stress manager, an NLP practitioner and a SIRPA practitioner. I offer 1-2-1 services to clients and workshops, to corporate companies, and I help people with stress, anxiety and chronic pain. That's way too many variables, it would be too confusing and too expensive to market each separately.

So by focusing instead on the customer and my foundations I was able to build something cohesive and much simpler. Here is what I offer, I am a mindset specialist (one) helping professionals to overcome stress, anxiety and chronic pain (many). Boom, simple. I don't market myself as all those different services, I don't offer them to everyone and see who comes in, my services are either corporate wellbeing workshops or 1-2-1 programmes and all of my marketing spend goes to the corporate/professional market.

How are you going to focus your business so that you can create cohesive customer journeys and allow yourself to work smarter not harder?

What keeps your clients awake at night?

Now that you have more clarity on your particular business structure and niche, you can focus on the particular customers you are going to serve and ask yourself, what keeps them awake at night? What is it that these clients particularly struggle with or feel frustrated by?

Understanding this allows you to choose solutions which

really speak to your audience e.g. if you want to work with teenagers with anxiety. What particular things do they struggle with? Put yourself in their shoes and list them.

For example perhaps one thing is that they have racing thoughts that they are falling apart and will be this way for the rest of their lives.

Creating a list of what keeps your clients awake at night gives you lots of inspiration for online creations. For example, you could create a video or blog about this particular topic, you could create a 5 steps e-book to help them stop racing thoughts, you could also use 'stop racing thoughts' in your landing page as an outcome for an upcoming 5-day programme. Teenagers with this particular struggle will then resonate with this content and feel like you understand them.

Knowing how your customer feels and what particular things they are struggling with, gives you lots of insights into what solutions you could create and helps you to create things they would actually want.

Think about your customers, put yourself in their shoes, where are they when they first start looking for your services and note down what they are struggling with, feeling, thinking etc. I've created a download sheet for this - if you want to use my template; you can download it here: http://bit.ly/Blueprint-Resources

If you are struggling to think about what your customers may be frustrated by or struggling with you could find out via market research. The exercise below will help you.

NOTE: Now I know many people suffer with imposter syndrome, and I resisted this activity for years. As part of the research, you are going to come across other people who do what you do and every time I looked at other people's work, I felt like I wasn't good enough, or I was never going to make it, or I thought what was the point when there were so many other people who could help. This is the wrong way to approach this activity and held me back for years!!! Unfortunately for me, I thought I knew my customer well enough to make a good guess. I was wrong! I've included some advice for anyone who suffers from imposter syndrome below the exercise.

What is already available in the market ?

I invite you to be curious about your industry and your client. This is not to compare yourself or your services to what's out there. This is for you to put yourself in your customers' shoes, get to know them more and understand their struggles or reactions to the services offered already. You're educating yourself about your customer so you can create something amazing and something which is perfectly you.

My 3 step Market Research download is available if you would like to print it so you can make notes. You can download it at **http://bit.ly/Blueprint-Resources**

Market Research exercise

Step 1

Join a relevant Facebook group relating to your topic and be a detective, what questions are people asking? What struggles do they talk about?

DO NOT get drawn into the group and lose 3 hours by answering people's questions, remember you are the detective. You are just gathering information.

Step 2

Go to Google, type in what your client may type and see what comes up. Do a little searching, look at the different options and note what you like and don't like.
DO NOT compare yourself to the services which come up, they may have been in business longer, they may have a team of people which you don't (YET). In this exercise you are just gathering information.

Step 3

Ask your current clients. If you are already established and have clients which are in your target customer group, you can ask them. Perhaps you'd like to invite them to a forum one evening or ask your questions on your social media. Sometimes offering a prize draw can encourage people to take part.

Once you have compiled your market research, I recommend you have a break. Then come back. Ask yourself the following questions and note down your findings:

- What excites you, is there anything you would love to create?
- What annoys you, are there any issues you'd like to resolve?
- What does your customer want answers to? What are they looking for?

- What specific language do they use when they express their struggles/frustrations?

**Suggestions for those who struggle
with imposter syndrome**

If, like me, you struggle when doing this exercise, I recommend that you do the following:

1) Limit the amount of time you spend on market research, do small bursts often rather than hours in one go.
2) Use affirmations to settle yourself and reaffirm you're good enough, capable enough and know enough to succeed. Use these before, during and after any market research activity.
3) Take plenty of deep breaths. Deep breaths help to calm your nervous system so if you notice your chest getting tight just pause and breathe.
4) Remember, what makes your business unique is you and there is only one of you, so people may be doing the same thing, but they won't do it the same way as you.

You can absolutely succeed in your business and I'm with you every step of the way. This research isn't about you, it's about understanding your customer.

Capture your findings, we will be using these when we move onto the next chapter and begin to create your structure.

Where do they live?

Thinking about where your customers live is an important question to ask yourself.

Sometimes a business is structured to serve a local market, this is especially true if you currently have a 1-2-1 face to face business. Adding online solutions doesn't necessarily mean you have to serve a wider market: you may want to create additional services for the same market. An online membership option for your current clients is an example of this. If you have a physical clinic or other premises you may want to continue to serve your local audience, just create more ways to offer them your expertise.

Alternatively, you may be looking into online solutions because you want to reach a wider market, perhaps there aren't enough people locally to make your business structure work. Or perhaps you have a dream of serving people from around the world and having an international company?

Working through this Blueprint is all about working smarter not harder and finding your natural passion and motivation. This way you can build a brilliant business but stop giving yourself a hard time whilst doing it.

I used to think I needed an international company to make my dreams a reality but recently I've changed my perception. Sometimes going too big can have a detrimental impact on your confidence and lead to you procrastinating. There are nearly 70 million people living here in the UK!! Depending on the customer/market you decided on earlier in this chapter there may be plenty of opportunities in your country. If people come to me from other countries that's fine, I'll serve them, but I don't have to over-face myself with the idea of building an international mega-business or focus my marketing spend on lots of countries. I can focus myself on the UK, knowing that I can achieve my money goals here. It felt like a weight had been lifted when I stopped giving myself such a hard time and realised, I could be 'successful' at a pace which felt more achievable.

Remember, your Blueprint needs to come together like a jigsaw so think about what you need in order to make your foundations work, given your time, money and passions. Note down where your customers live? Where is the market you're going to target? What market will give you enough scope to allow you to be successful given the choices you've already made with regards to time, money and niche? There is no right answer: here it's about playing with all the pieces until they fit.

What is common in that marketplace right now?

In section 1 you did your first bit of market research, in that exercise we focused on the customer and their current experience. In this section we're going to focus on the market as a whole and see if there are trends or opportunities which you would like to fill. Here we'll be building on what you've found already.

For this exercise it helps to step back from your business and think about it as a bigger picture, from a global perspective. What happens currently in the market as a whole? If you don't know, do some market research to find out. I've included an example below to explain the idea and help you to get started.

If my business supported women with anxiety, what would they do? They would probably go to their GP, perhaps get some medication, be given an opportunity of CBT perhaps, google for some books on the topic, ask their friends about ideas, Google ways to help anxiety. Then struggle on the best they could. If they didn't resolve their issue, they may google anxiety support within their area, find some local practitioners and take a big leap of courage and book in with one.

You may find that someone is offering some group anxiety support sessions in your area, have a look at who they target for customers, do they go for health prac- titioners, or companies etc. How often do they run the groups? Is it a webinar once a month? A small class of 10 people a week??

All of this is great information. It will help you to:

a) ignite your passion for a difference you want to make in the market
b) decide what your customers need/want from your business (you don't need to reinvent the wheel all the time!!)
c) spot opportunities to do something you and your customers would love.

Remember, there is enough room in the market for you. If you struggle with imposter syndrome whilst doing market research, go back to the tips I shared earlier in the book.

If you offer a great customer service for a topic you gen- uinely care about, people will get to know, like and trust you.

Once you've gathered your market research, ask yourself where are the opportunities in the market?

1) Your offer - Perhaps you'd like to offer something which doesn't currently exist, or to people who aren't served by the existing offers.
2) Your personality - perhaps you'd like to offer a different personality because everything on offer feels the same or isn't authentic to you.
3) Your marketing – perhaps looking at the market gives you ideas about videos/blogs your customers would read or ideas of how you could talk to these clients.

For the above example you may like to create an online anxiety bootcamp for women or a 5-day anxiety course for beginners. You may choose to use swearing and a direct no nonsense approach rather than the nicey, nicey stuff. You may decide to write an e-book about the current research, common signs of anxiety and share your top 5 tips. There's lots of inspiration to be found by understanding your customer and the current market.

Go and have a look at the market you wish to be in, be curious about what's out there and what your customers want. Stepping back from your business and observing the market as a whole can be a wonderful source of inspiration.

OK, so you should have lots of information about the customer and market you wish to serve. I hope this section has helped you to identify your customers and what business structure is going to work for you. And I hope that you have found these exercises more beneficial than the usual 'ideal client' questions.

Your place in the market

Another decision which is far more useful than your client's hair colour is where in the market your service is going to fit. I use a supermarket analogy to explain this one. In every market there are solutions for a budget audience, solutions for the everyman and solutions for the luxury client. You can definitely see this in the supermarket options available in the UK we have Aldi at the budget end, Tesco in the middle and Waitrose at the top for example. I'm sure you'll have similar options in the country where you live.

Here are three common problems I see in the helping professions. All of which can be solved by thinking and choosing where in the market your business is going to sit:

1) No decision at all
   People in the helping professions often don't make a decision at all when it comes to which segment of the market they wish to serve. This leads to endless procrastination and confusion. They often worry about making the wrong decision so instead don't make any. Their offerings become lost in an overcomplex business structure with no clear definition between their services and who they are for.

2) Offering too many options
   If you offer 3 or 4 services to a budget market, another 3 or 4 to the medium and another 3 or 4 to the luxury market you end up spinning too many plates and not getting any of them right. Remember, we are aiming to work smarter not harder. Simplifying and focusing would actually help you

achieve better results.

3) A luxury service to a budget customer
I see this overpromising issue with so many businesses. I get it, most people in our industries are
natural people-pleasers who care. You want to
give every client your best, but this business model isn't sustainable or profitable, you end up being
incredibly busy for not enough money. It's also
hard to sell: imagine offering a luxury mince pie
which costs £3 to someone in a budget supermarket - they wouldn't buy it.

Perhaps after reading this you're starting to spot some
of the things you're doing in your business. It's OK and
that's exactly why I'm here. It's OK to make mistakes, it's
how we learn so don't feel bad. I hope these revelations
help you to understand where you are right now and enable you to make different decisions which allow you to
move forwards.

If you have realised that you haven't chosen your strategy when it comes to your place in the market, here are
some options for your business:

Option 1 - Choose one and base your whole business on
serving this one level of client. The supermarkets do this
brilliantly, they know their audience and deliver exactly
what they want at the prices they can afford.

Option 2 - Design certain products in your range for certain
markets. Consultants often do this; you can buy a book
sharing their expertise and if you want their 1-2-1 services
it will be a premium offering at a premium price.

Think about your current business, do you want to have a business which serves one particular level of the market or do you want to create a business with a cross section of products for each one?

Newsflash: your Blueprint can change over time, a revelation I know, so don't put yourself under too much pressure. Instead choose what you can do now, think about what you like, then go with that. The Blueprint provides you with a structure so you can play with the 4 steps until you find something which works for you. You can absolutely review it over time and change it accordingly.

The choice is yours, but you do need to choose. Note down your preferences at this stage, we'll use these then we move on to creating your structure.

Before we move on, I wanted to make a note on branding. I recommend considering the look and feel of your business alongside this supermarket analogy. For example, if you decide to be a luxury business who serves luxury clients, the logo, feel and price should match. I want to help you to build a brilliant business so considering your branding could give you some insights into how you want to build your business going forwards.

A note about awareness

Another factor to consider is the level of awareness your clients have. In many markets there are people who are at the beginning of the journey, who are very unaware e.g. people with anxiety who don't know that's what the problem is. There are also people who are more aware e.g. people who know its anxiety and are now researching the different options. Finally, there are people who are very aware e.g. they've been reading the books, know exactly what they want and are looking for a solution which matches this requirement.

Why is this important? Because you can create online resources which match the different levels of awareness on the same topic. You may like to create something for people who are just starting out on their journey, answering their basic questions or you might want to focus your business on only people who are aware that your service is the answer. Again, the choices are up to you and part of the blueprint is playing around with these ideas to find the best matches for your business. If you're going to create online solutions which people will actually buy you need to know what awareness level they have and at what point in your business you will cater for this.

Chapter Summary

I know that there is a lot to consider in this chapter and I don't apologise for that. This chapter is where most businesses fail. If you don't spend time thinking and making conscious choices of who and how you're going to serve your customers you end up wasting time, money and effort creating things which people don't want.

The traditional "ideal client worksheet" rests on a great concept, knowing your customer is an important aspect of any successful business but I don't think the usual questions are particularly helpful. Instead, focus on creating a sound business structure, understand what your client's frustrations are, where in the market you want to be and how you can make an impact on these people.

Above all, build a cohesive journey for your customers taking them through your solution/s step by step from wherever they are now, to wherever they want to be. To do this you need to understand where they are now and the current market.

Sometimes defining these things takes time so, if you need to put the book down and work on this section for a while before moving on that's completely normal. Also, in my experience you learn more and more as you go along your business journey, so some people keep coming back to this chapter and honing it as they go. That's absolutely fine too.

Perhaps you've never thought about any of this before and it's given you a clearer direction of where to start or maybe you've already defined your customer/market but now feel you want to make some changes. So long as the 4 steps of your Blueprint fit together feel free to play with this until you find what works for you.

Chapter 5

Building your structure

"Logic will get you from A to B. Imagination will take you everywhere."

- Albert Einstein

O K so now you have your solid foundations in place, and you have defined your environment/market, it's time to start deciding what things you're actually going to create and building your structure.

Yes, we need to be logical, your structure needs to fit with the two steps of the Blueprint you've worked on so far, but this is where we also need a good dose of imagination and creativity. Without that we end up creating boring solutions which don't get us excited about our businesses or excite our customers to consume them.

Here is a reminder of the four step Blueprint. In this chapter we're moving onto step 3 so here's a more detailed image of what this step entails.

2. Environment/Market

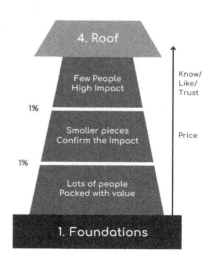

Like many others, early in my business I made one of the most common mistakes, I offered 1-2-1 services and I didn't pay much attention to anything else. The challenge is that there just weren't enough people being introduced at the bottom of my structure to get me enough 1-2-1 clients at the top. My marketing strategy required lots of my time e.g. going networking or writing continuous content and my 1-2-1 services took lots of my time too, there just wasn't enough of me to go around. I wasn't attracting enough people to convert into enough 1-2-1 clients.

I see the same thing happening with many service based/ helping professionals, they don't create something lower down, at the bottom of their structure, and they don't focus a proportionate amount of time on getting people to start their journey with them. People need to get to know, like and trust you and most customers aren't going to invest large amounts of money to do that. If people do create something at this lower level of their structure they choose something which takes an immense amount of their time like a Facebook Group or weekly blogging (or both!!). This leaves them with little time left for anything else. It's not you!!! Even the biggest names convert at 1%.

It's not you, I always thought I was doing badly when I offered an event and 3 people signed up. But, it's not you it's your numbers!! If you put an event out to 20 people, you'll get maybe 1 person interested. That's not you, doing something wrong, that's just fact. Even the biggest names who have made millions and have a 3   person marketing machine still convert online at about 1%. And, a cold audience i.e. people you have no contact with are harder to convert because they don't know you.

So many service/therapy businesses struggle at the beginning because they underestimate how much it takes to let people know who you are and what you have to offer. Back to a point I made earlier, doing an online talk to 20 people is not going to convert to 24 customers a quarter!!! You are more likely to get 1 client and going by the 1% rule that would be a good outcome.

I once went to an event about marketing by JTFoxx, an American multi-millionaire and during this event he shared his numbers. This was a free 1-day event in Manchester. He'd had about 70,000 people say they were interested, around 700 sign up and 176 actually there on the day. And, this was classed as a really successful event which was run by a full marketing team!!! He didn't even give us the numbers of how many people had looked at this initial marketing ad/content and were not interested!!! 70,000 people interested, 176 actually there, that's a conversion of 0.25%. Free events often have a higher no-show rate so it's not surprising that this was less than the 1%.

Another issue I see a lot of people doing is offering their 1-2-1 services right off the bat, this is too big and often potential clients don't know you. Sure perhaps 1 person who is really desperate will say yes but that isn't going to build you a sustainable business.

The opposite, but equally big issue is I see a lot of people do too much in their bottom/lower tier, they do a blog, a free webinar, a Facebook Group, a free download and sometimes even more. Each time they meet people they're talking about something different. That's way too much for you to consistently keep up with and too much for your clients to know what the next steps are that they need to take. They're almost waiting for next week to see what else they can have for free.

You have to choose something you can create once and talk about often and spend your time and money on getting those well-chosen things in front of the eyes of lots of people.

Remember the important rule I shared with you when we started looking at your environment/market, you want to lead your customer on a journey, starting from where they are and leading them through a sensible path to where they want to be. I hope that by now you're seeing how the Blueprint is beginning to fit together.

Expanding your thinking

So many people jump into their ideas too quickly without first exploring their options. As the title quote stated, if you only use your logic to create your structure, you'll create something which is obvious, and in many ways quite dull and unexciting. So, before you decide on your structure, I encourage you to engage in some creativity. If creativity really isn't your forte bring a few friends together, particularly choosing some who think differently to you.

Within the boundaries of your foundations and your environment/market decisions explore what is possible. Have fun, engage in free thinking, no option is too big, too crazy, too stupid. It's this creative flair that ignites our brains and this is where our lightbulb moments come from. Nothing new was created by thinking only logically about a problem.

Using your structure, your personality, your flair, your ideas for changing the world what possibilities are there for you to create. Sure you could create an e-book but what makes that e-book something you are excited about creating and something your clients will want to read?

OK, so I know there will be some people who get stuck

here because they have barriers to creativity or perfectionistic tendencies. Remember, at this stage we are focusing on generating ideas - it's a chance to think about something in a different way. I know you may want to 'get it right' or you think this activity is just a nice/fun thing to do but it isn't. This is based in neuroscience and the way our brains work. We have two sides to our brains, one logical, one creative so why only use half of your brain to find your ideal solution? Also, forget about the technology for now, I can help you with that, for now focus on ideas and really enjoy the freedom this type of thinking creates.

Seriously, do this!! I promise it will give you renewed energy and excitement for your business. What do you need to do to make this happen? Perhaps schedule some time in your calendar right now, perhaps reach out to a friend and ask when they are free? Start, do something to get this started right now.

Grab some paper and some pens and let yourself (or your group of friends) have some free thinking/creating time. You may be amazed at what ideas you come up with. You can then channel those into workable things using the ideas I share below.

It's not the video, e-book or course which is the solution, these are merely the vehicles you use to get your ideas over to the customer, it's the enthusiasm, passion and connection which are important.

Your structure is what creates the customer's journey. To create a coherent business structure we are going to create online things which fit into the Blueprint's low, middle and high tiers.

- The low tier- Items here are designed to connect with lots of people and encourage them into your

services. These will help the customer to understand your expertise and connect with you.
- The middle tier – Anything here is designed to be the next step on the customer's journey, they will be priced higher and help to build that know, like and trust factor. They could serve a part of the market which wouldn't afford your high option or provide a fully online version rather than your 1-2-1 service for example.
- The high tier – These are your platinum or premium offers. At this point people know, like and trust you, they want to work with you in a dedicated way and therefore the price is high and you'll work with fewer people.

Next, we'll take the ideas you generated earlier and map them into these tiers. This enables you to create a cohesive customer journey in line with your foundations (step 1) and environment/market (step 2) of the Blueprint.

Ideas for low tier online creations

OK so now you have been creative and tapped into the part of your brain that unleashes your best ideas, it's time to hone them into something more logical.

I want you to refer back to your foundations and how much time you actually have to spend on your business. I also want you to look at your audience and decide what they would love to have available to them at the beginning of their journey. Remember things at this low level need to attract lots of people and begin your conversations with them.

Once you have those elements in mind look at your list of ideas and my list of ideas below and choose something which excites you to do, is reasonable and sustainable given your time considerations AND is enticing for your audience.

1) **A book/e-book** – something you create once and sell many times. It can help you to create a voice of authority within your industry and introduce people to your concepts.

2) **A challenge** – something simple they can do each day or something you can take them through step by step. Challenges are a great way to get people started, there could be a week challenge on a specific step or a social media post each day. These have been a huge success with the ice bucket challenge, the 100happydays challenge etc. You'll need to put it out too MANY people but it should be a no brainer for your customer to sign up too.

3) **A webinar** – similar to a challenge a webinar is an online event where people get to join you and learn something simple. Don't over promise!!! Just something to get them started. These are a great way to spend 1 hour with people and really help them to get to know you. MANY people, 1 hour of your time.

4) **A video or email series** – these are things which people sign up to and receive a video or email each day helping them along. These can be pre-recorded or written and then run over and over again.

5) **A blog/vlog/podcast** – regular content sharing your thoughts, ideas and tips with your audience.

Think very carefully about your choice here. Choose 1! Maybe 2 at a push if you're full-time and really savvy in terms of time management. Your Blueprint needs to fit together like a jigsaw, your foundations, environment and structure.

My thoughts on Facebook Groups

This seems to be the in thing to do, there are literally thousands of them. I get the idea, you set up a group, spend time building it by nurturing your audience and then convert them into customers. But there are lots of challenges with this.

1) The market is saturated, there are so many Facebook groups your customers are probably part of about 200 different groups. How many invites to Facebook groups do you receive? Do you have time to be actively involved in these groups and have a life!! In my experience only a few groups stand out so if you're going to do it, it has to be amazing.

2) To build an audience on Facebook is a time-consuming task. Unless you already have a huge audience and you're just looking for somewhere for them to communicate together. Starting a Facebook Group from scratch requires you to be in there talking, posting and drumming up conversation constantly. People underestimate how much time it will take.

3) Conversion: how are you going to convert that group into customers? Why would they sign up when they're already getting so much of you for free? Getting customers from Facebook groups isn't always easy. Facebook groups by design are a

place to meet and chat not to sell. Too much sales talk in there and you'll lose your audience.

4) Politics: With a group of people comes the need to manage that group of people. You'll need to spend time administrating the group, deleting unrelated posts, mediating fall outs between members, managing opposing viewpoints etc. Once again, all this takes time!!

When a Facebook group is the right option

There are times when a Facebook group is the right option.

1) When you already have a large audience of people e.g. Facebook page and you want to bring them together in a way which is easier to access.

2) When you have a stand-out topic which is perfect for general chit chat style conversation (again I would only do this if you have a large network of people.)

3) When you have a paid-for programme and as part of that programme you want somewhere for people to communicate together.

4) When you are big enough to have a marketing team and the free Facebook group is something they can admin and feel this is a good addition to your marketing strategy.

Middle tier

The middle layer is for products/programmes which aren't your full offer. They are the next level of commitment and set at a higher price. People who like you will want more of you so what could you put together so they can get to know you even better?

Mistakes here are often related to over commitment. Your best work and time should be reserved for your highest-level customers so look at your foundations and decide how much time you have to dedicate to these middle layer offers.

Remember my points earlier about where in the market you want your business to be - we used the supermarket analogy. If you can't remember go back and review your decision there. Perhaps these middle layer offers are your budget options for those who can't afford your full consultancy. Or perhaps you have decided to focus on the luxury market and these offers are their lower-level treats, demonstrating your service and dedication.

Ideas for your middle tier:

1) **A mini online course** – a course for those who can't afford your consultancy where you go through things with them online.
2) **A video/email series** – particularly if your lower layer is an e-book, the video series could go into more depth.
3) **An event** – an evening or half day smaller priced event which you only do a few times.
4) **A membership/group programme** – you could do a weekly coaching session for a group of people.

Remember to be thoughtful about the amount of time and the amount of information you give at this point. These are mid-layer offers so should receive a related amount of your time. Don't be giving your luxury opportunities for a mid-layer price.

You'll convert 1% of the people from your lower levels into these mid-layer offers so how many people would you need in order to make your finances work?

High level tier

At the highest tier you want your clients to receive the most amount of your dedicated attention and the most amount of support. This layer is often your 1-2-1 consultancy offer. If they want your dedicated help and the best service, they pay a higher price. You will want only a few people to commit at this level so that you have the time to serve them.

Again, don't over-stuff your offer at this point, I've seen countless people throw all sorts of courses, content, sessions etc into this offer and much of it the customer doesn't value. Go back to looking at who your customer is and think about what they would consider to be the best, most amazing service. You may be surprised to find that the little things which don't take much are what they would actually value the most.

Ideas for your high tier:

- 1-2-1 sessions
- Online course with coaching support
- Mastermind group with 1-2-1 support

Take some time now to begin to build your structure. Think carefully about how you can bring the elements of the Blueprint together. You need a structure which matches your foundations and your environment/market. It's no good throwing together some brilliant ideas and hoping for the best. Be strategic in your choices and you can build a brilliant business where your online solutions not only enhance your business but save you time and money.

A few examples to get you started.

1) A chiropractic clinic.

Low Tier - They have a process in place so that each member of the team takes it in turn to blog. These blogs go out weekly to their newsletter audience. An audience they've built from their client list. They also go out on their website, social media and they have ads on Facebook and Instagram to deliver them to new people within the local area of the clinic.

Middle Tier - They have created an online resource centre for members. People pay a monthly fee and on top of their 1-2-1 sessions they have access to courses online about some complementary things, discounts on block bookings and resources which they can download like exercise worksheets with videos of how to complete them. They also hold an annual xmas lunch which is discounted for members.

Top Tier - The top-level tier is their 1-2-1 sessions in the clinic with their staff. The clinic also has an online induction programme for all of their staff ensuring their customers receive a high level of service.

2) A therapist who works with anxiety.

Low Tier - This therapist has an e-book explaining anxiety, it's symptoms and giving some simple steps the clients can take at home. Once a month they also go live on their Facebook group talking with someone who experiences anxiety.

Middle Tier - They have an anxiety-at-home online programme with resources a client can use e.g. audios, books they can read and 5 strategies they can implement to lower their anxiety at home. They have set up automated emails to check in with these people as they go along and upsell the 1-2-1 programme if they need more help.

High Tier - They have a 1-2-1 programme which consists of a number of 1-2-1 sessions plus they have weekend retreat events for people with anxiety which they run twice a year.

3) A high-end consultant who helps people with grief

Low Tier - On their website they have a free video series explaining the grief process, people can sign up at any time and over the following week they receive a video each day with a task for them to complete that day. It teaches them what to expect and also links to videos of people's stories.

Middle Tier - They have a grief mastermind group, bringing people together who are going through the same experience, this includes a group where they can talk, and the consultant goes live into this group once a week to offer guidance and support. There is also an online platform sharing resources and an opportunity to 'upgrade' to a 1-2-1 programme if they feel they need it.

High Tier - They have a 6-month consultancy offer which supports that person every step of the way. It also includes email support and some little touches along the way like flowers sent to the house or a card/note to say they're doing well.

Chapter Summary

Your structure is where everything starts to come together, you want to choose pieces which strategically fit with both your foundations and your environment/market. Remember that even the experts convert at 1% so often it's not you or your ideas which are the issue, it's your numbers. Often we are just being busy fools, trying everything and hoping that something sticks, don't do that!!! Instead, create a structure in 3 tiers featuring offers at low, medium and high tiers and create an effective journey for your clients through those tiers. You want to build the know, like and trust factor as you move up through the structure along with increasing the amount of dedicated time they have with you and therefore the price they pay.

Chapter 6

Topping out

"Everyone faces defeat. It may be a stepping-stone or a stumbling block, depending on the mental attitude with which it is faced."

- Napoleon Hill

n building terms topping out is when the last roof truss has been secured into place. It's the moment you officially have an actual building. In terms of building a brilliant business this section is the one which most people miss.

Before we get started, let's have a reminder of the 4 steps of the Blueprint:

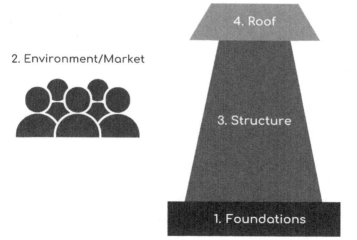

Introducing the Roof

In this section we're going to be working on the 4th section, which I have called the Roof.

In order to secure your structure, you need to finish it with a strong roof. We do this by reviewing, revisiting and revising our creations and strategy. So many people think of a brilliant idea, create the whole thing and when only 5 people signup they ditch the whole thing and do something entirely different

So many people start doing online weekly vlogs but after 3 or 4 months give up because they don't have an audience of millions (I've done this one!!)

Often your idea is a sound one: you just need to test your audience, test your images, test your wording and tweak it to the things which work best. As Napoleon said, see it as a stepping-stone. Perhaps you need to add in another email or connect with a slightly different audience. Perhaps your landing page needs some work, or you need to work on your marketing because you're not connecting with enough people. Your roof needs to be secure in order to build a brilliant structure.

Consistency is rewarded, show up, keep showing up and keep tweaking until you hit gold. Don't create 6 different ideas and ditch each one when floods of people don't sign up. Don't create a webinar, do it once and then because you don't get any clients create a completely new one from scratch. Here is my Roof Checklist to help you to work smarter, check these things before you ditch a product/offer and create a new one:

Roof Checklist:

1. The audience:
   - Who is my audience for this particular product/offer?
   - Do I need/want to tweak who this is for?
   - Does my marketing reach out to enough people in this market?
   - Is the price point congruent with this audience?

2. The messaging
   - Am I hitting the concerns and wishes of the audience in my posts and landing pages?
   - What images am I using, do they connect with the messages I'm trying to portray, are they compelling, and do they reflect my brand?
   - Am I marketing this offer/product well? Am I putting my messages out there and would people know what this is about?
   - Does the booking experience flow, am I communicating well all the way through the journey, including before, during and after the event?

3. The content
   - Does the product/offer reflect value at the price point I have set?
   - Does the content match where the customer is at or am I over-delivering/overwhelming the customer with my content?
   - Is my content answering the audience's

concerns/problems/wishes?
- o Is my content easy to understand for my audience?
- o Does the content's look and feel match my brand?

This is by no means an exhaustive list, but it gives you some key questions to review. If you feel something needs tweaking, try it and see what difference it makes. A note of caution though, don't change too many things all at once, you won't know which changes have created the results. Quite a few systems allow you to do something called split testing which means you can create different things and show each one to a portion of the market. I did this recently by creating two different landing pages for an event to see which one performed better. You can also do this with adverts on social media so you can test different text and image combinations.

Overcoming Perfectionism

I, like so many others, am a recovering perfectionist. I used to want everything to be perfect before I launched it, I had to get the content right, the price right. I would spend hours creating and thinking until I thought I had something wonderful. What happened was that my ideas ended up being what I thought people wanted and never really fit with the audience's needs. This led to them being met with rather a lukewarm response. Now I ask my audience, I connect, and I talk to them more. I then use their ideas as a base. I have my 3-tier structure in place which allows me to know what level an idea or products would be and at what price point I'm aiming at and then I pilot an idea. I offer it out and ask some people to be part of the pilot. This way whatever works grows into something amazing, whatever doesn't I tweak or remove. I save so much time and money doing things this way.

You can trial ideas before you build them. I did this with my membership package, I sold it with the understanding that the people who signed up would be helping me to build something amazing. It didn't exist as more than an idea when people signed up. I knew where it sat in my structure but I needed people to work with so I could create something great.

It doesn't have to be perfect; it doesn't even have to be written, it just needs to be a strategically sound idea. Then launch it and allow your audience to become part of its creation. They'll tell many more people about it if they have been involved in creating it AND it takes the pressure off you.

With my marketing pieces I come up with something and then test, test, test. I change the pictures, change the text, change the audience and then focus on the ones which convert the most.

Remember you will convert at 1%, your ideas aren't wrong, often you just need to tweak them and tell more people about them. This is Topping Out!! The final step in the blueprint.

CASE STUDY

I started in 2011 as the Wedding Karma, helping people lose weight, speak with confident and overcome their nerves. I booked a number of wedding fayres and in the first 12-18 months of my business I helped 2 people. I had created the website, the leaflets, the branding and even spent a lot of money on a business coach to work out the text on my landing pages. The whole business earned me about £500 and cost me a hell of a lot more. After 18 months I threw in the towel. Looking back, here were my mistakes.

I didn't take time to understand the market or listen to how they needed the support. I thought I knew best. I was newly qualified as a hypnotherapist, I looked around at what other hypnotherapists did and did the same: I offered my 1-2-1 support by the hour for £60. Yes, people wanted help to lose weight and talk with confidence, but when planning a wedding they had limited money and no free time, both of which I hadn't factored into my business concept. My concept was too time consuming and too much money, it was floored before I started. What would you spend an extra £200-£300 on if you were getting married, the dress, the flowers or some sessions to lose weight? Most people have overspent on the dress, flowers, rings and everything else before they even start!!!!

The roof of the Blueprint

I did zero of this!!! I came up with an idea, went out to market and when it didn't work threw in the towel as a bad idea. I then created Refreshed Minds with a new website, new leaflets, new branding etc. I had wasted money, a whole lot of time and felt like I was a failure.

If I was going to set up this business again, I'd do it very differently. I'd implement the 4 steps of the Blueprint. Oh, the joy of hindsight! I now have so many ideas of things I could create to make the Wedding Karma business work. And, I certainly wouldn't have thrown in the towel on all that hard work just because something didn't work the first time. I'd have tried things out before spending so much on marketing and I'd have consulted the audience much more so I could create a solution which they actually wanted. Lessons learnt!! I hope these help you to not fall into the same trap I did. Or to correct it before you decide to give it all up and try something completely different.

What things should you review?

Have a look at your business currently and ask yourself what needs tweaking, testing or reviewing? Perhaps you have some courses you created ages ago which didn't sell, or you have a programme which people only complete 10% of on average. Perhaps you created an event but only a few people signed up or you had some ideas but never actually put them out into the world.

In light of your newfound knowledge of the Blueprint and all the work you've done as you've gone through this book, ask yourself the following questions:

1) Why didn't this work? Perhaps you need to tweak the audience or send it out to more people?
2) Did you do any testing/tweaking at the time, if so, what were your numbers? What are they telling you?
3) How do you feel about the creation/event now? Do you feel you threw in the towel on a good idea, or that it doesn't fit at all in the structure you've now created?

4) Could you update your idea to work within your new structure/decisions? Perhaps you could change the price or change the offer to fit better into your Blueprint structure.
5) What could you try now and what testing would you do as you go forwards?

Not only is the roof a good place for reviewing your existing ideas but also an important part of any ideas going forwards. Perhaps, like me you're a recovering perfectionist and realise now that you really need to put something out there and not hold back until it's perfect. Giving yourself permission to tweak and test as you go along can be wonderfully freeing. Knowing that you don't have to get something perfect first time releases the pressure and allows you the freedom to be creative and try things.

I know that this can feel scary but honestly the minute that I stopped worrying so much about getting things right, and instead opened up to my customers about my ideas, they started getting excited, cheering me along and asking if I could help them. Nowadays I put the bare bones of something together or better still sign people up and then create it, tweak, change and tune as I go. I put a little marketing spend towards an idea, test a few different things and then go with the one which works the best. I ask more, I try more and ultimately I am more successful because of it.

Chapter summary

How many times have you created something, had a few people sign up and then ditched the whole thing as a bad idea? You are not alone and this is often what people do. The final stage of the Blueprint is the roof and this is where you test, review and refine. Allowing yourself to let go of perfectionism and instead asking your audience, giving something a go and allowing yourself permission to tweak and change things along the way. Perhaps you already have some great ideas you could review and revamp, perhaps you need to tweak something in a creation you are currently offering. Review the audience, the messaging and the content using the Roof Checklist and you may be surprised how easy changes can improve your outcomes.

Chapter 7

How to implement the Blueprint

"The secret of getting things done is to act!"

- Dante Alighieri

You came to this book wanting to consider how to build your business by serving people with an on-line offering. You may have come to this book with expectations about what that delivery would look like and for this book to be a manual of how to build it e.g. a step-by-step script for making your Facebook group into a money earner? Remember the thing which makes your business unique is you, but it's not you that fails - it is often the structures that underpin your ideas and your business. With this Blueprint you can revisit the 4 steps as many times as you want, reviewing and re-evaluating your choices, ensuring they all fit together and so enabling you to build a brilliant business.

If you have been dipping into the book or reading the full content before trying out the exercises, I implore you to start now on your own Blueprint by following the activities one at a time. You can read all the business self-help books in the world, but the magic happens when you actually do the work and apply it. This Blueprint isn't an idea you can read and just mentally process. It's a business model to implement and build on throughout your business journey. I encourage you to put some time in your diary right now and work on the activities so you can build the Blueprint for your own business.

How to Overcome the Fear

I know that getting started with online technology can feel daunting. I hear so many people say they're 'no good' at technology. This isn't true by the way, it's just that you haven't been shown yet. We all start off with zero knowledge and grow from there over time, it's called the learning ladder.

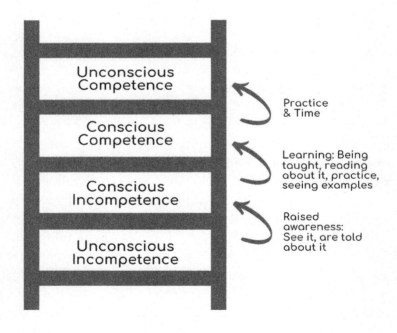

We start off being blissfully unaware and quite happy not knowing about things and not having the ability to do them, this is what we call being unconsciously incompetent. For example, when we are babies, we have no concept of driving and we don't get agitated about our inability to drive.

We then move into conscious incompetence. This is where you are consciously aware of something, but you can't do it, for instance you can be aware that there's technology which can help you, but you don't know how to use it. At this stage everything can feel scary, you look at people, like me, who can create, record, edit and share a video in an hour and you feel like there's a huge chasm between your reality and theirs. Because of this you feel dumb, stupid and procrastinate constantly about getting started. Often there is a desire and a want to do it, but you are afraid you'll make mistakes.

The next level of the learning ladder is conscious competence. At this stage you are aware there's the technology to help you, and you have begun your journey to learning it, but it takes concentration to do it and feels exhausting. To get to this stage you have to give yourself permission to learn. This stage takes patience, a trait which many people struggle with then it comes to their own learning journey.

Finally, with practise, you move up the learning ladder to unconscious competence, this is where you do things without even thinking about it.

If you compare yourself to others and always seem to come up short, I completely understand. Comparing myself with others was a mindset I struggled with for many years and still do sometimes. We forget that everyone has their own learning ladder and that they too started off where you are now. Contrary to popular belief, I'm not a natural at technology, I didn't just pick up a video camera and start creating amazing content. I've learnt this stuff over years and years of practise. I've read instruction booklets, pressed buttons, made mistakes, lost hours of work in a flash due to not pressing save, spent hours playing about with various systems, created hundreds of videos...and because of that it now looks like I do it effortlessly - most of the time!! I have finally reached the stage of unconscious competence, but I certainly didn't arrive here by accident or purely because of some inherent 'talent.'

The good news is you don't need to know everything I know to get started. You can absolutely start with something simple and learn as you go. You can focus on your own learning ladder and take it step by step; you may be surprised by what you become great at!

I hope that this Blueprint will ease your levels of concern and worry because it gives you a structure to follow, helping you feel confident with your own ideas. But I wouldn't be doing you justice if after many years as a private therapist I didn't give you my top tips to overcoming fear. If you are struggling to get started and feel stuck by fear, below are my 3 top tips:

3 top tips to overcoming fear:

1) It's okay to feel fear

The feelings of fear are not life threatening, just because your heart pounds and you sweat doesn't mean the thing you're doing shouldn't be done. It also doesn't mean that you have to create a life which avoids this feeling at all costs. Living a life purely in your comfort zone feels boring, uninspiring and doesn't give you the opportunity to feel the elation of achieving something.

My tip? Reframe your mindset so that fear isn't something bad. The feeling of fear is necessary, and it can be exhilarating!!

2) Fear is often false

Fear comes from our ability as a human being to project into the future and into the past, and letting our heads become filled with "what if's" and "maybe's". For example, what if this goes as bad as last time, what if people don't like it etc. Our brains are trying to keep us safe by filling our mind with questions hoping that the answers may help us to avoid peril. But this strategy isn't based in logic or truth, instead it's based on endless irrational thoughts and usually they are playing on our biggest values and concerns.
My Tip? Fear isn't based in the present and it's not based in actual truth - if you focus your mental energy on the present or the truth, you usually feel much calmer.

3) You are more capable than you think

You would be amazed at how strong, resourceful and resilient you can be in the moment. We spend so much time putting ourselves down and being our own worst critic that we start to believe it. What if you built yourself up instead of tearing yourself down? What if you focused on what you've achieved rather than all the things you haven't? What if you stopped assessing your weaknesses and spent time doing things which matched your strengths?
My tip? A mindset shift towards showing yourself compassion and kindness can have a huge and powerful impact on your own perspective, and what you're capable of.

The Blueprint and beyond

Now it's time to decide on your own Blueprint, to plan your actions and help you to move forwards. Below is an action plan to help you to implement the Blueprint into your business. I have also created an action plan download so if you would like a template to complete you can find that here: http://bit.ly/Blueprint-Resources

Choose your next 3 priorities

Diving into new things can seem like there's lots to do so by focusing on your next 3 priorities you can get started on something tangible. Your priorities should be things you can actually do, don't go too big and then get over-whelmed and don't go so small and feel uninspired. So what will be your next 3 priorities? Here's some ideas:

- Complete the activities in this book.
- Decide which elements of the Blueprint you already have in place and which you feel need more work.
- Review your current products/offers in line with the Blueprint.
- Conduct some market research to understand your audience and market.
- Gather your thoughts on your structure and choose what things you're going to focus on at each level.
- Break down the content and messaging for your first product/programme/course.
- Learn how to create your first product/programme/course.

Choose your 3 top priorities right now and schedule

them into your calendar - with reminders - so you can get them done.

Imagine what you could achieve in the next 6 months with your Blueprint in place, imagine how you could change people's lives for the better, including your own.

I've given you a great structure to start from and build on, and I understand that it's not always easy to put yourself out there or get to grips with technology, but you can absolutely do this, and you don't have to do it on your own.

If you would like help with the technology using quick and simple videos: sign up to my AMA (Ask Me Anything). **https://builditbrilliant.co.uk/ama**

AMA subscribers can ask me questions via email and each week on Friday at 10am I'll send you a video answering questions from that week. You can also subscribe to my YouTube channel, as 8 weeks later I release the videos on there. So this is a great way to access videos sharing various hints and tips and refer back to them time and time again.

If you'd like more ongoing support as you build your Blueprint, join as a Build It Brilliant (BiB) member. This means you'll have:

- Accountability - myself and other members are there to keep you on track.
- Support – like-minded people to bounce your ideas off and share your journey with.
- Expertise - more comprehensive resources to teach you the technology and overcome the mindset blocks as you go.

You can become a BiB member here: **https://builditbrilliant.co.uk/membership**

Through the BiB Membership I'm building a community of helping professionals who want to share their journey with other like-minded people and learn together. It doesn't matter where you are in your own journey, whether you're a complete beginner or more advanced, there's so many options in the online world we can learn together. This is a welcoming and structured space where you can take things at your own pace and build your confidence as you go.

If you would like to go VIP and work with me more closely, exclusively on your business on a one-to-one basis, I'd like to invite you to book in for a Discovery Call with me: **https://calendly.com/zoethompson/discovery-call**

And as for me?

I'm super proud of myself for writing this book and putting my Blueprint down in words so that many more people in the helping professions can build brilliant businesses. Every day I imagine the positive impact that could have on the world!!!

I have some more exciting things in the pipeline including appearing in podcasts, more speaking engagements and exhibiting at conferences - you never know, you might bump into me in person. I'm also looking forward to welcoming more people as BiB members and creating resources and courses to help them achieve their dreams. Finally, I will also be out on my motorbike, experiencing even more wonderful adventures.

I'm looking forward to hearing about your journey to building a brilliant business, I'd love to hear from you so

pop over to my Facebook page and tell me more about it:
www.facebook.com/BuildItBrilliant

   Welcome to the wonderful world of online creations,
here's to overcoming our mindset blocks, getting out
there and building a brilliant business.

Zoe.

Zoe is passionate about helping those who make a positive difference in the world to grow their confidence in using online technology so they can reach a wider audience and build a brilliant business. Zoe has 10 years of experience building and implementing e-learning for multinational companies and 9 years of experience building her own private therapy business. She is logical and creative, energetic and organised. Zoe will help you to build online solutions which you will be excited to create and your customers will be inspired to consume.

Facebook @BuildItBrilliant
Instagram @builditbrilliant

www.builditbrilliant.co.uk

Printed in Great Britain
by Amazon